D1328197

Major Systems
of the Body

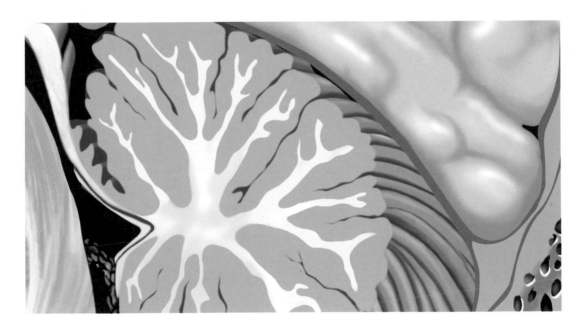

WORLD ALMANAC® LIBRARY

Please visit our web site at: www.worldalmanaclibrary.com
For a free color catalog describing World Almanac® Library's list of high-quality books and multimedia programs, call 1-800-848-2928 or fax your request to (414) 332-3567.

The editors at World Almanac® Library would like to thank Dr. Ron Gerrits, Assistant Professor of Biomedical Engineering, Milwaukee School of Engineering, for the technical expertise and advice he brought to the production of this book.

Library of Congress Cataloging-in-Publication Data

612
MAJ
2002

Major systems of the body.
     p. cm. — (21st century science)
    Summary: A description of the structure and function of major systems of the human body.
    Includes bibliographical references and index.
    ISBN 0-8368-5007-6 (lib. bdg.)
    1. Human physiology—Juvenile literature. [1. Human anatomy. 2. Human physiology.] I. Title. II. Series.
  QP37.M346 2002
  612—dc21
                                                   2002021193

This North American edition first published in 2002 by
World Almanac® Library
330 West Olive Street, Suite 100
Milwaukee, WI 53212 USA

Created and produced as *The human body* by
QA INTERNATIONAL
329 rue de la Commune Ouest, 3ᵉ étage
Montreal, Québec
Canada H2Y 2E1
Tel: (514) 499-3000 Fax: (514) 499-3010
www.qa-international.com

© QA International, 2002

Publisher: Jacques Fortin

Editorial Director: François Fortin

Executive Directors: Stéphane Batigne, Serge D'Amico

Illustrations Editor: Marc Lalumière

Art Director: Rielle Lévesque

Graphic Designer: Anne Tremblay

Writers: Stéphane Batigne, Josée Bourbonnière, Nathalie Fredette

Computer Graphic Artists: Jean-Yves Ahern, Pierre Beauchemin, Maxime Bigras, Yan Bohler, Mélanie Boivin, Jocelyn Gardner, Danièle Lemay, Alain Lemire, Raymond Martin, Annie Maurice, Anouk Noël, Carl Pelletier, Simon Pelletier, Claude Thivierge, Michel Rouleau, Frédérick Simard

Page Layout: Véronique Boisvert, Geneviève Théroux Béliveau

Researchers: Kathleen Wynd, Jessie Daigle, Anne-Marie Villeneuve

Copy Editor: Jane Broderick

Translation: Käthe Roth

Production: Mac Thien Nguyen Hoang

Prepress: Tony O'Riley

Reviewers: Dr. Alain Beaudet (Department of Neurology and Neurosurgery, McGill University), Dr. Amanda Black (Department of Obstetrics and Gynaecology, Queen's University), Dr. Richard Cloutier (Département de dermatologie, Centre hospitalier universitaire de Québec), Dr. Luisa Deutsch (KGK Synergize), Dr. René Dinh, Dr. Annie Goyette (Département d'ophtalmologie, Centre hospitalier universitaire de Québec), Dr. Pierre Duguay, Dr. Vincent Gracco (School of Communication Sciences and Disorders, Faculty of Medicine, McGill University), Dr. Pierre Guy (Orthopedic Trauma Service, McGill University Health Centre), Dr. Michael Hawke (Department of Otolaryngology, Faculty of Medicine, University of Toronto), Dr. Patrice Hugo, Dr. Ann-Muriel Steff (Procrea BioSciences Inc.), Dr. Roman Jednak (Division of Urology, The Montreal Children's Hospital), Dr. Michael S. Kramer (Departments of Pediatrics and of Epidemiology and Biostatistics, Faculty of Medicine, McGill University), Dr. Pierre Lachapelle (Department of Ophthalmology, McGill University), Dr. Denis Laflamme, Dr. Maria Do Carmo (MD Multimedia Inc.), Dr. Claude Lamarche (Faculté de médecine dentaire, Université de Montréal), Dr. Sheldon Magder (Faculty of Medicine, McGill University), Dr. Nelson Nadeau, Dr. Louis Z. G. Touyz (Faculty of Dentistry, McGill University), Dr. Teresa Trippenbach (Department of Physiology, McGill University), Dr. Martine Turcotte, Dr. Michael Wiseman (Faculty of Dentistry, McGill University).

World Almanac® Library Editor: Alan Wachtel

World Almanac Library Art Direction: Tammy Gruenewald

Cover Design: Katherine A. Goedheer

Table of Contents

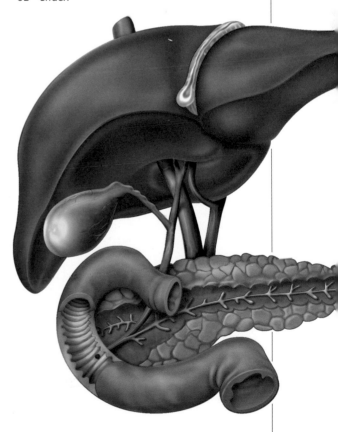

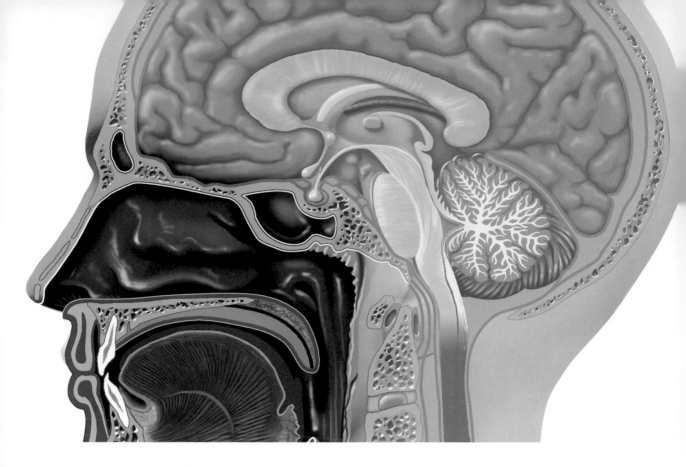

Like all living organisms, the human body needs certain substances to survive and develop. Two major systems supply it with the substances needed by its metabolism: the respiratory system and the digestive system. Respiration brings oxygen from the air into the bloodstream, while digestion is the process by which the body absorbs nutrients from food.

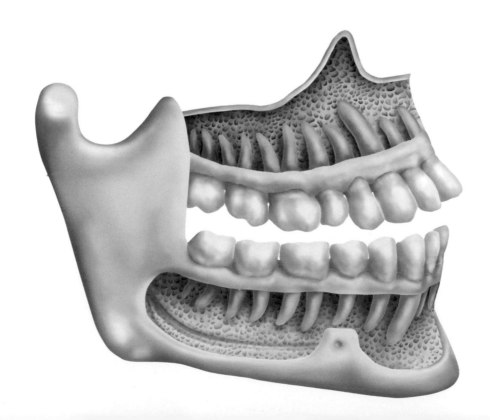

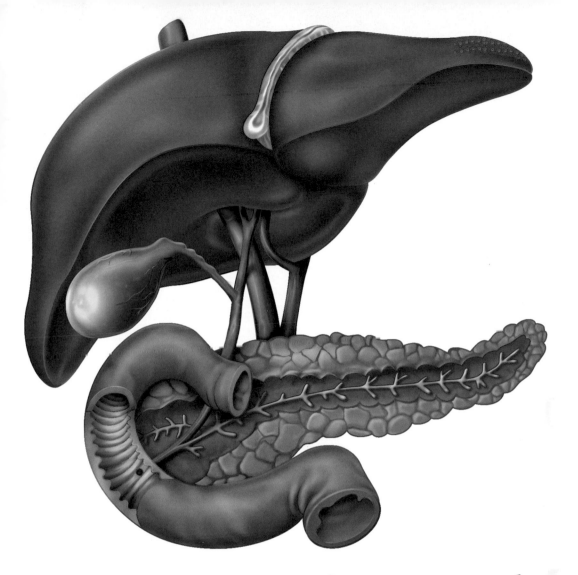

Respiration and Nutrition

The Respiratory System
Oxygenating the body

Because the cells that make up a human being die if deprived of oxygen, the body must constantly breathe, oxygenating itself through the process of respiration. This generally involuntary process, which is governed by specialized neurons in the brain stem, consists of bringing air from outside the body to the depths of the lungs via the branching network of the lower airway system. These numerous branches make up most of the mass of the lungs, which are the main organs of respiration.

THE ORGANS OF RESPIRATION

The respiratory system is composed of a series of airways that transports air from outside the body to the alveoli of the lungs, where gas exchange occurs. The upper airway is composed of the nasal cavities and the pharynx. The lower airway is composed of the larynx, trachea, bronchi, and lungs.

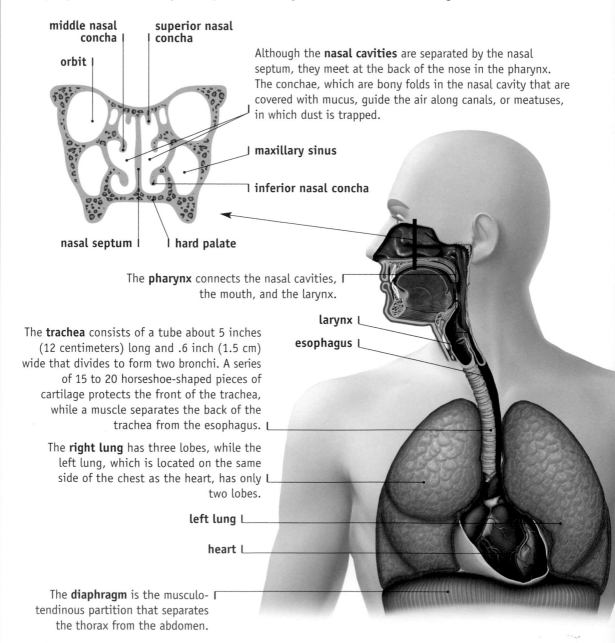

middle nasal concha **superior nasal concha**

orbit

Although the **nasal cavities** are separated by the nasal septum, they meet at the back of the nose in the pharynx. The conchae, which are bony folds in the nasal cavity that are covered with mucus, guide the air along canals, or meatuses, in which dust is trapped.

maxillary sinus

inferior nasal concha

nasal septum **hard palate**

The **pharynx** connects the nasal cavities, the mouth, and the larynx.

larynx

esophagus

The **trachea** consists of a tube about 5 inches (12 centimeters) long and .6 inch (1.5 cm) wide that divides to form two bronchi. A series of 15 to 20 horseshoe-shaped pieces of cartilage protects the front of the trachea, while a muscle separates the back of the trachea from the esophagus.

The **right lung** has three lobes, while the left lung, which is located on the same side of the chest as the heart, has only two lobes.

left lung

heart

The **diaphragm** is the musculo-tendinous partition that separates the thorax from the abdomen.

THE LUNGS

The trachea divides into two primary bronchi, each of which leads to one of the two lungs. These channels, in turn, subdivide into secondary bronchi that lead to the lobes of the lungs. In the lobes, they divide into tertiary bronchi, which branch into narrower, even more numerous bronchioles. This branching structure is known as the bronchial tree.

The inside of the **trachea**, like the rest of the bronchial tree, is covered with a ciliated mucous membrane that directs impurities to the outside. The point at which the trachea divides into the left and right primary bronchi is known as the carina.

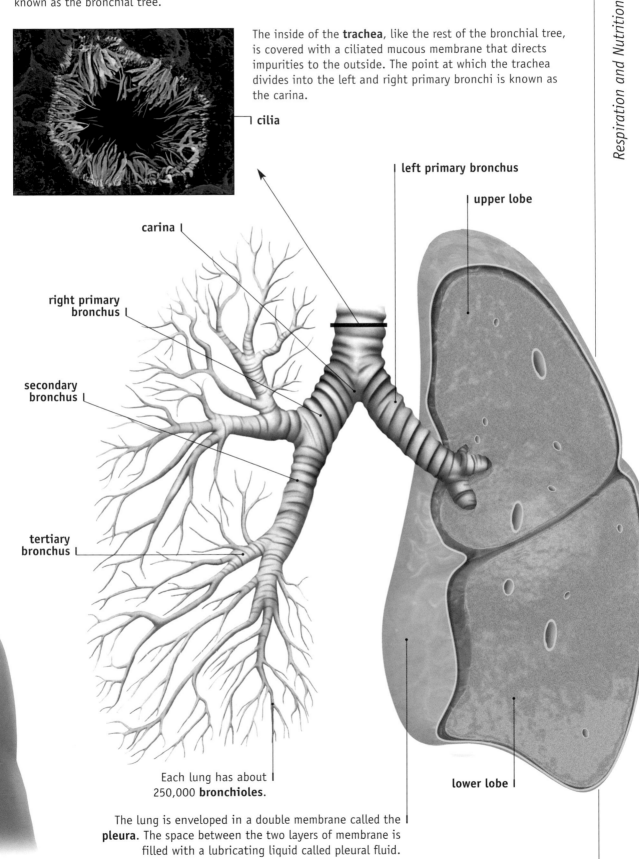

cilia

left primary bronchus

upper lobe

carina

right primary bronchus

secondary bronchus

tertiary bronchus

Each lung has about 250,000 **bronchioles**.

lower lobe

The lung is enveloped in a double membrane called the **pleura**. The space between the two layers of membrane is filled with a lubricating liquid called pleural fluid.

Respiration

Exchanges between air and blood

The diaphragm and the intercostal muscles work together to cause inhalation, or the pulling of air deep into the lungs. In contrast, no muscle work is needed for exhalation, in which the body expels carbon dioxide made by its cells. At the ends of the bronchial tree in the lungs are the pulmonary alveoli, which are tiny air sacs that are in close contact with blood capillaries. There are so many alveoli that their total area is more than 1,000 square feet (100 square meters). It is along their surfaces that gas exchanges between air and blood take place.

INHALATION AND EXHALATION

The coordinated activity of the diaphragm and the intercostal muscles inflates the lungs. During the inhalation phase, the diaphragm ❶ and the intercostal muscles ❷ contract. Their contraction enlarges the rib cage and increases the volume of the lungs ❸. The difference in air pressure in the lungs before and after the contraction draws air in through the trachea ❹. Exhalation, on the other hand, is an essentially passive phenomenon, caused by the elasticity of the rib cage as the diaphragm and intercostal muscles relax.

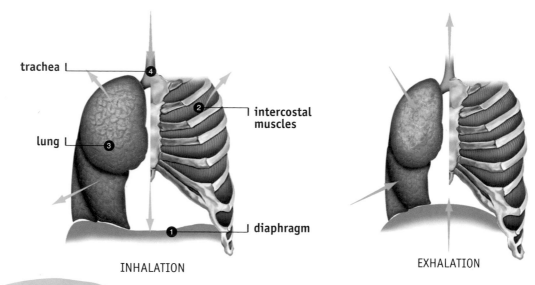

trachea

intercostal muscles

lung

diaphragm

INHALATION

EXHALATION

The **sinuses** are cavities in the facial bones that heat the inhaled air and contribute to vocal resonance.

nasal cavity

nostril

THE ROLE OF THE NOSE IN RESPIRATION

Inhaled air enters the body through the nostrils and crosses the nasal cavities on its way to the pharynx. As it passes through, air is filtered by the hairs in the nose, which hold back large dust particles. The mucus that lines the nasal cavities also traps undesirable particles and helps humidify the air passing through. Finally, tiny blood vessels in the nose warm cold air before it reaches the lungs.

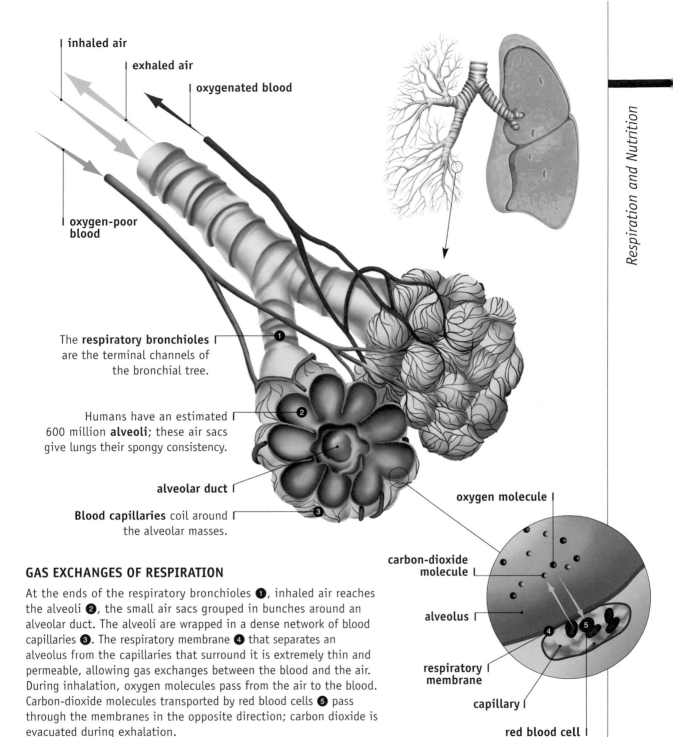

inhaled air

exhaled air

oxygenated blood

oxygen-poor blood

The **respiratory bronchioles** ❶ are the terminal channels of the bronchial tree.

Humans have an estimated 600 million **alveoli**; these air sacs give lungs their spongy consistency. ❷

alveolar duct

Blood capillaries coil around the alveolar masses. ❸

oxygen molecule

carbon-dioxide molecule

alveolus

respiratory membrane

capillary

red blood cell

GAS EXCHANGES OF RESPIRATION

At the ends of the respiratory bronchioles ❶, inhaled air reaches the alveoli ❷, the small air sacs grouped in bunches around an alveolar duct. The alveoli are wrapped in a dense network of blood capillaries ❸. The respiratory membrane ❹ that separates an alveolus from the capillaries that surround it is extremely thin and permeable, allowing gas exchanges between the blood and the air. During inhalation, oxygen molecules pass from the air to the blood. Carbon-dioxide molecules transported by red blood cells ❺ pass through the membranes in the opposite direction; carbon dioxide is evacuated during exhalation.

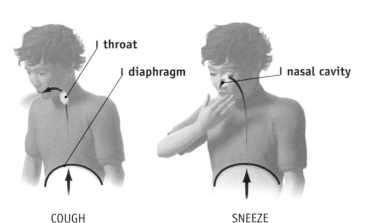

throat

diaphragm

nasal cavity

COUGH

SNEEZE

COUGHING AND SNEEZING

When particles obstruct the airways, special respiratory actions are spontaneously triggered to expel them. Coughing clears the bronchi, trachea, and throat, while sneezing produces a powerful current of air in the nasal cavity. It is estimated that sneezed air is expelled from the body at speeds of over 90 miles per hour (150 kilometers per hour)!

Speech

Vibration, resonance, and articulation

Humans produce many different speech sounds—the phonetic elements of a language—that they form into words to express themselves. This ability is the result of a complex interaction between the brain, the lungs, the larynx, the pharynx, and a collection of mobile articulators that includes the tongue, lips, lower jaw, and soft palate, also called the velum. The lungs and larynx provide the sound source for human speech, while the upper airway, known as the vocal tract, shapes the sounds they produce.

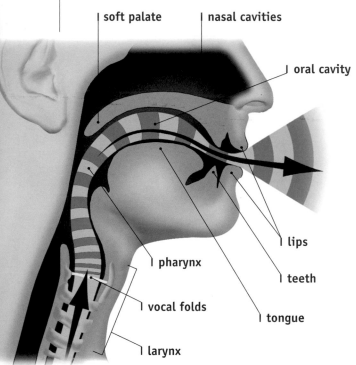

- soft palate
- nasal cavities
- oral cavity
- lips
- pharynx
- teeth
- vocal folds
- tongue
- larynx

THE PROCESS OF SPEAKING

If the vocal folds are close together, pressure supplied by exhaled air vibrates them, producing a tone. This process is called phonation. The size and shape of the vocal tract, which is controlled by the positions of the mobile articulators, amplifies certain frequencies of the tone. The vocal tract can change shape to make many complex sounds; these various sounds make up the phonetic elements of language.

Attached to the mandible by muscles and tendons, the **hyoid bone** supports the larynx.

The **epiglottis** is a cartilaginous flap that covers the larynx during swallowing to keep food from entering the lungs.

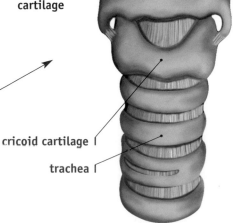

- thyrohyoid membrane
- thyroid cartilage
- cricoid cartilage
- trachea

THE LARYNX

The larynx is the part of the upper airway situated on top of the trachea and opening into the pharynx. It is made of pieces of cartilage linked by ligaments and muscles, and it is covered by mucous membranes. The largest of these pieces of cartilage, the thyroid, forms a visible bump in the neck in men called the Adam's apple. The vocal folds are within the thyroid cartilage.

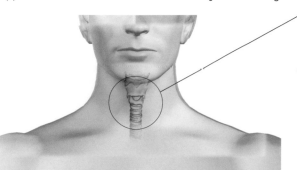

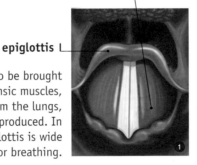

epiglottis

vocal folds

THE VOCAL FOLDS

The vocal folds are long, smooth, rounded bands of muscle tissue that can be lengthened or shortened, tensed or relaxed, and separated or brought together. They are attached to the thyroid cartilage in the front and to the arytenoid cartilage in the back. Activation of the various intrinsic muscles, which are also attached to the arytenoid cartilage, causes the vocal folds to open wide during respiration. The same muscles close, tense, and stretch during phonation. For sound to be made when exhaled air passes through the vocal folds, the edges of the folds must be more or less closed; the amount of closing affects voice quality.

thyroid cartilage

arytenoid cartilage

The **posterior cricoarytenoid muscle** causes the vocal folds to separate.

The **lateral cricoarytenoid muscle** causes the vocal folds to meet in the midline.

The **cricothyroid muscle** stretches the vocal folds, making the voice rise in the pitch.

In general, men's **vocal folds** are longer and more massive than women's; this is why men tend to have lower voices.

The **glottis** is the space between the vocal cords.

Phonation ❶ requires the vocal folds to be brought closely together. The tension of the intrinsic muscles, along with the pressure applied from the lungs, determines the quality of the sound that is produced. In contrast, no sound is produced when the glottis is wide open ❷ and the larynx is used solely for breathing.

epiglottis

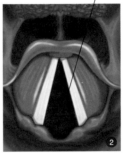

ARTICULATION OF CONSONANTS AND VOWELS

A large number of muscles act to position the tongue, lips, jaw, and soft palate in various shapes in order to articulate different consonant and vowel sounds.

Many **consonants** result from the obstruction of air flow by the tongue, lips, teeth, and hard palate, sometimes working together. Occlusive consonants (p, t, k) are produced by the complete obstruction and then sudden release of air flow, while fricative consonants (f, th, s, sh) are produced by an incomplete obstruction, resulting in noise-like sounds. Voiced consonants—b, d, g, v, z, and j—are produced while the vocal folds are vibrating, using either complete or incomplete obstruction of air flow to form their sounds.

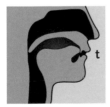
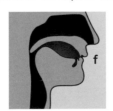

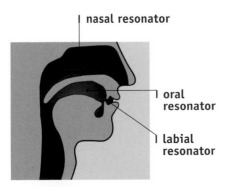

nasal resonator

oral resonator

labial resonator

Articulation of **vowels** involves no major obstacles to the passage of sounds from the larynx to the mouth opening. The most important factors affecting vowel articulation are the size and shape of the vocal tract, the degree of lip rounding, and the degree of muscular tension. Changes in the oral, labial, and nasal cavities also contribute to vowel articulation. In some languages, such as French, the nasal resonator is involved in articulation of nasal vowels when the velum of the soft palate moves to let some air pass through, adding a nasal quality to the sound of these vowels.

The Digestive System

How foods are transformed and absorbed

The energy that the human body needs to function is supplied by food. Working together, the organs that make up the digestive system decompose food, absorb its nutrients, and eliminate waste material. The series of conduits and pouches through which food travels before being evacuated in the form of fecal matter is called the digestive tract. This 30-foot- (9-meter-) long tract starts at the mouth and continues, in order, through the pharynx, esophagus, stomach, small intestine, large intestine, rectum, and anus.

Some related organs contribute to digestion although they are not part of the digestive tract. The teeth and tongue help to transform food into alimentary boluses. The salivary glands, liver, pancreas, and gallbladder all produce or store digestive substances—including enzymes—and release them into the digestive tract where they help to break down food.

THE PATH THAT FOOD TAKES

We begin to transform the food we eat in the mouth, where the teeth grind it up, the tongue compacts it, and saliva moistens it. Amylase, a digestive enzyme contained in saliva, begins to break down sugars. In less than one minute, the mouthful of food has become an alimentary bolus ❶—a soft, moist ball.

Swallowing requires perfect coordination of the muscles of the mouth and pharynx. The tongue pushes the alimentary bolus to the back of the mouth, where it enters the pharynx. At the same time, the tongue raises toward the soft palate, which obstructs the nasal cavity and keeps the bolus from entering it. As the bolus slides into the pharynx ❷, it pushes the epiglottis down, closing the entrance to the trachea. The pharynx and tongue combine to propel the alimentary bolus down the esophagus.

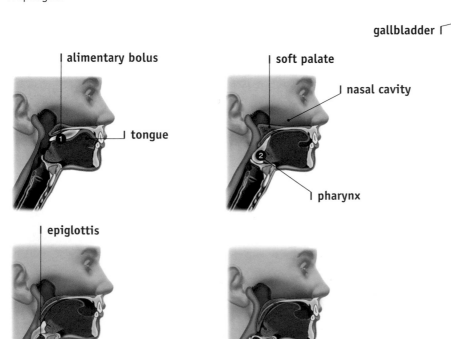

gallbladder

alimentary bolus

soft palate

nasal cavity

tongue

pharynx

epiglottis

trachea

esophagus

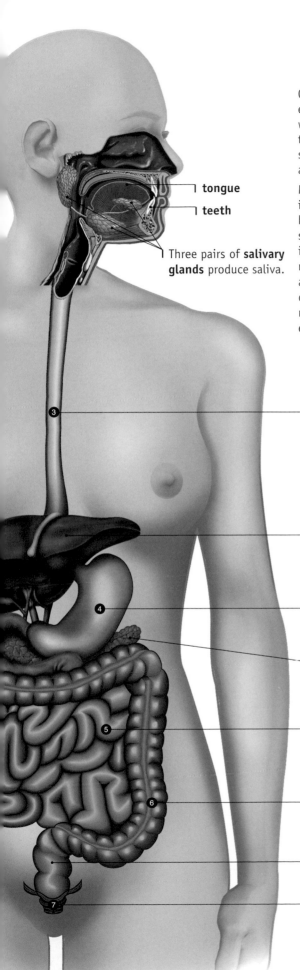

tongue

teeth

Three pairs of **salivary glands** produce saliva.

Once swallowed, the alimentary bolus descends the esophagus ❸ in a few seconds. It enters the stomach ❹, where it mixes with gastric juices containing enzymes that begin to decompose its sugars and proteins. This step, which lasts two to four hours, transforms the alimentary bolus into a substance called chyme.

Most digestion and absorption occurs in the small intestine ❺, where the chyme remains for one to four hours. Bile and pancreatic juices, released into the small intestine, completely decompose the food, and its nutrients are absorbed through the intestinal mucosa. In the large intestine ❻, where some water and ions are absorbed, the parts of the food that cannot be used by the body are transformed into fecal matter and then stored for at least 10 hours before being evacuated through the anus ❼.

The **esophagus**, which is a tube about 10 inches (25 cm) long, propels the alimentary bolus to the stomach through a series of involuntary muscular contractions called peristalsis.

The **liver** is the largest organ in the human body except for the skin. It contributes to digestion by producing a number of substances.

The **stomach** can hold around 4 quarts (4 liters) of food.

The **pancreas** controls the sugar level in the body and releases digestive substances.

The **small intestine** looks like a folded inner tube. It is between 13 and 23 feet (4 and 7 m) long.

Unusable remains from chyme are transformed into fecal matter in the **large intestine**.

rectum

The sphincters that surround the **anus** relax to permit defecation.

The Teeth

Getting food ready for digestion

Before gastric and intestinal juices decompose it, food undergoes a physical transformation in the mouth. Mastication, better known as chewing, is the first step in preparing food for digestion. The teeth—numbering 20 in children and 32 in adults—fragment food so it can be further transformed in the mouth into a lubricated alimentary bolus that can be swallowed.

TYPES OF TEETH

Thirty-two teeth in total—16 in the upper jaw and 16 in the lower jaw—make up the adult human dentition. There are four different types of teeth: incisors, canines, premolars, and molars. Each type has a differently shaped crown and root, and each crown shape plays a specific role in chewing.

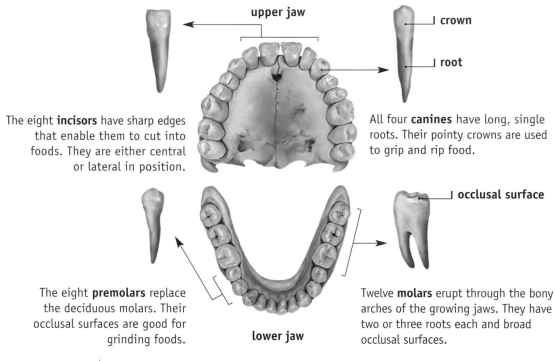

upper jaw

crown

root

The eight **incisors** have sharp edges that enable them to cut into foods. They are either central or lateral in position.

All four **canines** have long, single roots. Their pointy crowns are used to grip and rip food.

occlusal surface

The eight **premolars** replace the deciduous molars. Their occlusal surfaces are good for grinding foods.

lower jaw

Twelve **molars** erupt through the bony arches of the growing jaws. They have two or three roots each and broad occlusal surfaces.

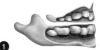
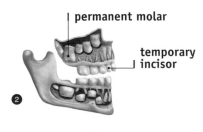
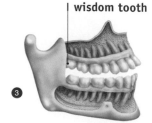

①

permanent molar

temporary incisor

②

wisdom tooth

③

DEVELOPMENT OF THE DENTITION

The formation of the teeth, which begins when the fetus is only a few weeks old, continues until adulthood. At birth ❶, the teeth are not visible, but the jawbones contain tooth buds that develop, grow, and, finally, pierce through the gums at 6 months of age.

By five years of age ❷, a child has 20 temporary teeth, also known both as milk teeth and deciduous teeth. This set of teeth includes eight incisors, four canines, and eight molars. The permanent teeth are already developing in the jaws, pushing toward the oral cavity and absorbing the roots of the deciduous teeth. Replacement of the temporary teeth by permanent teeth takes place over several years, generally between ages 6 and 12.

An adult's dentition ❸ consists of 32 permanent teeth. The four last molars, known as wisdom teeth, do not emerge before 17 years of age. Wisdom teeth can remain stuck in the jawbone if it does not grow large enough for them to fit behind the other molars.

THE HARDNESS OF TEETH

Permanent teeth, which appear during childhood, are durable enough to last for decades. They are hard and strong because of the kind of tissues of which they are made. Enamel, the teeth's protective coating, is a tissue made mainly of calcium phosphate and calcium carbonate; it contains less than 1 percent organic materials.

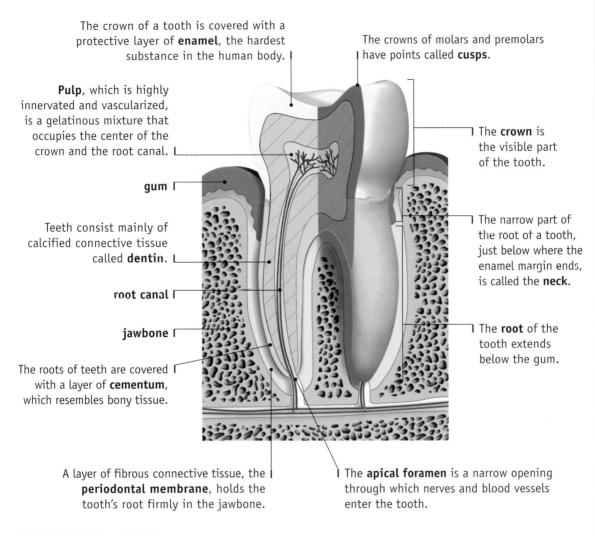

The crown of a tooth is covered with a protective layer of **enamel**, the hardest substance in the human body.

The crowns of molars and premolars have points called **cusps**.

Pulp, which is highly innervated and vascularized, is a gelatinous mixture that occupies the center of the crown and the root canal.

The **crown** is the visible part of the tooth.

gum

Teeth consist mainly of calcified connective tissue called **dentin**.

The narrow part of the root of a tooth, just below where the enamel margin ends, is called the **neck**.

root canal

jawbone

The **root** of the tooth extends below the gum.

The roots of teeth are covered with a layer of **cementum**, which resembles bony tissue.

A layer of fibrous connective tissue, the **periodontal membrane**, holds the tooth's root firmly in the jawbone.

The **apical foramen** is a narrow opening through which nerves and blood vessels enter the tooth.

TREATMENT OF A CAVITY

When bacteria attack the enamel of a tooth, they create a hole called a cavity ❶, which increases as the decay, also called dental caries, progresses through the enamel and into the dentin ❷. After drilling the decaying tooth to remove all traces of infection, a dentist fills the hole with a sealing compound ❸. If left untreated, the decay continues to propagate, infecting the living tissues in the pulp ❹ and sometimes forming an abscess ❺. If this problem occurs, a dentist must perform root canal therapy ❻ to stop the infection. This treatment consists of completely removing the pulp tissue from the tooth and then permanently sealing the root canals with an inert substance. Root canal therapy deprives the tooth of its innervation and blood vessels, but the periodontal membrane, root, and crown remain intact.

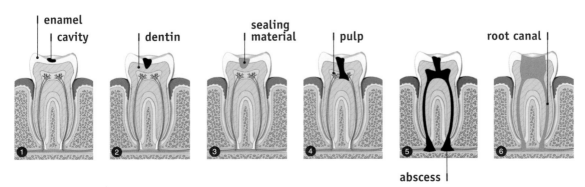

enamel
cavity

dentin

sealing material

pulp

root canal

abscess

The Stomach

A pouch with an acid environment

The alimentary bolus moves from the esophagus into the stomach, an elastic pouch about 10 inches (25 cm) long that secretes extremely acidic juices. Mixed together by the constant movement of the stomach's muscle layers, foods are slowly transformed into a mush, called chyme, that is expelled in small quantities into the duodenum of the small intestine.

THE MUCOSA OF THE STOMACH

The interior mucosa of the stomach consists of a layer of epithelial tissue that folds in on itself to form cavities called pits. This mucosa sits on a vascularized submucosa that covers three muscle layers. The fibers in each layer are oriented in a different direction to ensure that foods are well mixed. The gastric glands that are located in the stomach release different substances, such as hydrochloric acid, enzymes, mucus, and hormones, that combine to form gastric juices.

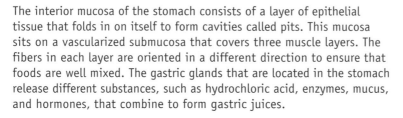

esophagus

The **pylorus** has a sphincter, or small ring-shaped muscle, that controls the exit of chyme from the stomach.

duodenum

The **mucosa** of the stomach includes many cavities, called pits, at the bottom of which are the gastric glands.

muscle layers

The stomach is covered by the **peritoneum**, a transparent membrane that surrounds all viscera.

The **gastric glands** produce a number of different substances, including hydrochloric acid, that sterilize and break up the alimentary bolus.

Separated from the mucosa by a thin layer of muscle, the **submucosa** of the stomach contains many blood vessels and lymphatic vessels.

THE GASTRIC CYCLE

When it reaches the stomach, the alimentary bolus is kneaded, mixed with gastric juices, and transformed into a whitish mush called chyme ❶. Regular contractions of the stomach push the chyme toward the closed pylorus ❷ at the bottom of the pouch. The sphincter of the pylorus opens periodically to release small quantities of chyme into the duodenum ❸.

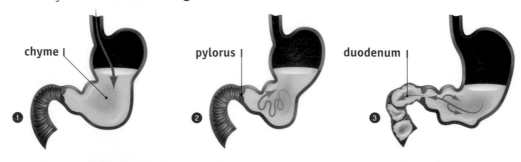

chyme

pylorus

duodenum

❶   ❷   ❸

The Intestines

A succession of tubes

After the stomach transforms the alimentary boluses into chyme, the chyme enters the intestines, which are the long series of tubes in which most of the digestive process occurs. The small intestine absorbs nutrients, while the large intestine transforms the chyme into fecal matter. Muscular contractions of the intestines evacuate the fecal matter through the anus.

THE SMALL INTESTINE

The small intestine is a very long, folded tube that consists of three parts—the duodenum, the jejunum, and the ileum. In this tube, intestinal juices secreted by its mucosa, pancreatic enzymes, and bile perform most of the digestive process. The small intestine also absorbs nutrients from the chyme through its epithelial cells. The many villi on the internal lining of the tube greatly increase the size of its absorptive surface.

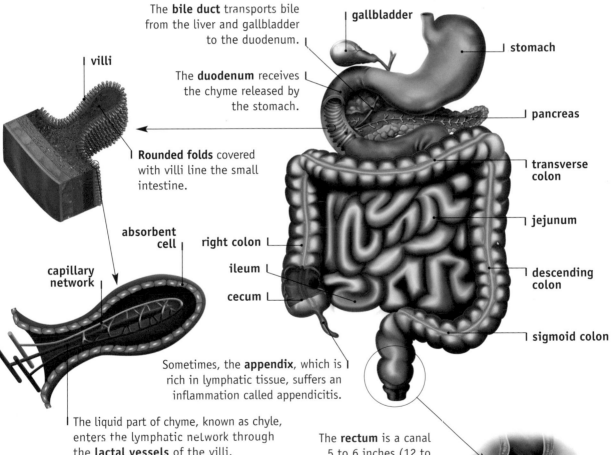

The **bile duct** transports bile from the liver and gallbladder to the duodenum.

gallbladder

stomach

The **duodenum** receives the chyme released by the stomach.

pancreas

villi

Rounded folds covered with villi line the small intestine.

transverse colon

jejunum

absorbent cell

right colon

ileum

cecum

descending colon

capillary network

sigmoid colon

Sometimes, the **appendix**, which is rich in lymphatic tissue, suffers an inflammation called appendicitis.

The liquid part of chyme, known as chyle, enters the lymphatic network through the **lactal vessels** of the villi.

The **rectum** is a canal 5 to 6 inches (12 to 16 cm) in length.

THE LARGE INTESTINE

The chyme passes from the ileum to the cecum, the first part of the large intestine. Then it moves to the colon, where bacteria complete its degradation. As water is absorbed by the mucosa of the colon, the chyme solidifies and is transformed into fecal matter. The colon pushes the fecal matter to the rectum, triggering the reflexive opening of the internal anal sphincters. The external sphincters, which can be contracted voluntarily, enable defecation to be controlled.

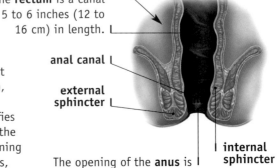

anal canal

external sphincter

internal sphincter

The opening of the **anus** is triggered by the internal and external sphincters.

The Liver, Pancreas, and Gallbladder

Biochemical laboratories

The digestive tract could not perform all of its functions without the assistance of certain organs related to the digestive system. The liver, pancreas, and gallbladder manufacture and store many digestive substances and then release them into the duodenum.

THE LIVER

The liver, which weighs over 3 pounds (1.5 kilograms), is the largest gland in the human body. Located on the right side of the abdomen, this organ consists of two asymmetrical lobes separated by the falciform ligament. The liver receives a large quantity of blood from both the hepatic artery, which comes from the heart, and the hepatic portal vein, which rises from the small intestine (1.5 quarts [1.5 l] per minute); because so much blood passes through it, the liver is involved in more than 500 different chemical reactions. In effect, it is a biochemical laboratory. Among other functions, the liver makes bile, cholesterol, and proteins. It also stores glucose, iron, and vitamins and degrades certain toxic substances that enter the blood, such as alcohol.

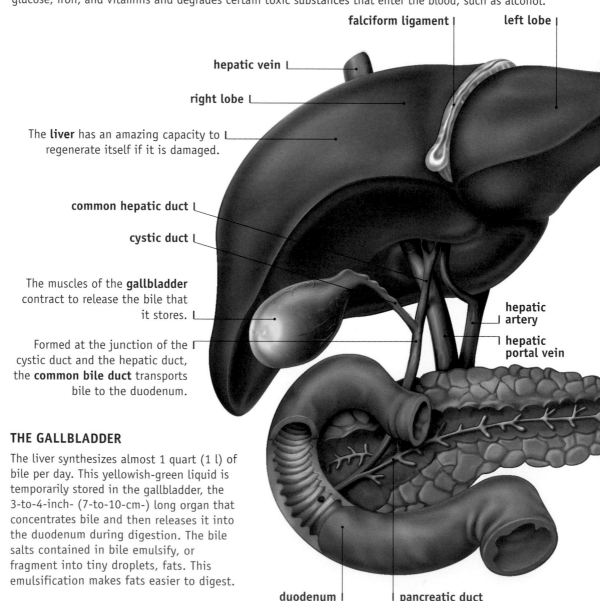

falciform ligament

left lobe

hepatic vein

right lobe

The **liver** has an amazing capacity to regenerate itself if it is damaged.

common hepatic duct

cystic duct

The muscles of the **gallbladder** contract to release the bile that it stores.

Formed at the junction of the cystic duct and the hepatic duct, the **common bile duct** transports bile to the duodenum.

hepatic artery

hepatic portal vein

THE GALLBLADDER

The liver synthesizes almost 1 quart (1 l) of bile per day. This yellowish-green liquid is temporarily stored in the gallbladder, the 3-to-4-inch- (7-to-10-cm-) long organ that concentrates bile and then releases it into the duodenum during digestion. The bile salts contained in bile emulsify, or fragment into tiny droplets, fats. This emulsification makes fats easier to digest.

duodenum

pancreatic duct

LIVER LOBULES

The liver is divided into hexagonal units, each measuring about .04 inch (1 mm) in diameter. These units, known as liver lobules, are made of specialized cells, called hepatocytes, that radiate out from a central vein. Branches of the hepatic portal vein and the hepatic artery supply the lobules with blood.

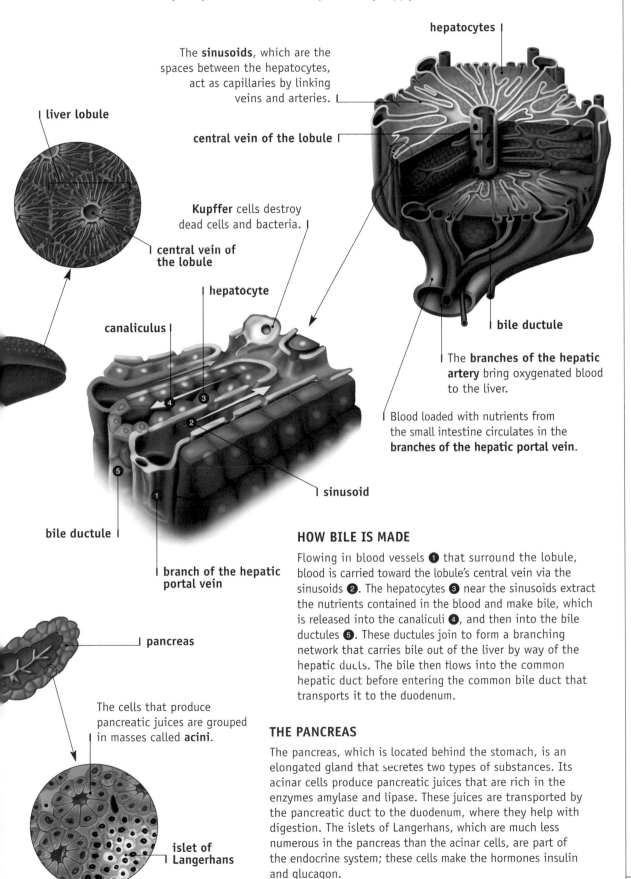

hepatocytes

The **sinusoids**, which are the spaces between the hepatocytes, act as capillaries by linking veins and arteries.

central vein of the lobule

liver lobule

Kupffer cells destroy dead cells and bacteria.

central vein of the lobule

hepatocyte

canaliculus

bile ductule

The **branches of the hepatic artery** bring oxygenated blood to the liver.

Blood loaded with nutrients from the small intestine circulates in the **branches of the hepatic portal vein.**

sinusoid

bile ductule

branch of the hepatic portal vein

pancreas

The cells that produce pancreatic juices are grouped in masses called **acini.**

islet of Langerhans

HOW BILE IS MADE

Flowing in blood vessels ❶ that surround the lobule, blood is carried toward the lobule's central vein via the sinusoids ❷. The hepatocytes ❸ near the sinusoids extract the nutrients contained in the blood and make bile, which is released into the canaliculi ❹, and then into the bile ductules ❺. These ductules join to form a branching network that carries bile out of the liver by way of the hepatic ducts. The bile then flows into the common hepatic duct before entering the common bile duct that transports it to the duodenum.

THE PANCREAS

The pancreas, which is located behind the stomach, is an elongated gland that secretes two types of substances. Its acinar cells produce pancreatic juices that are rich in the enzymes amylase and lipase. These juices are transported by the pancreatic duct to the duodenum, where they help with digestion. The islets of Langerhans, which are much less numerous in the pancreas than the acinar cells, are part of the endocrine system; these cells make the hormones insulin and glucagon.

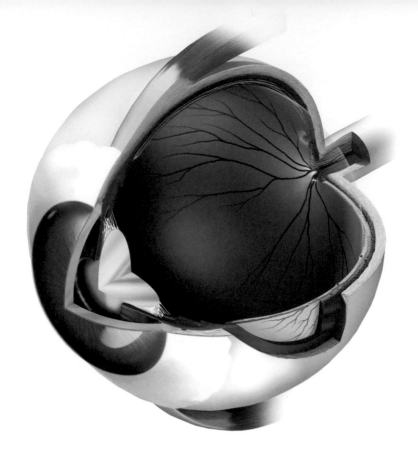

Touch, sight, hearing, taste, and smell—these are our five senses. We depend on these five complementary perception systems to learn about the world around us. The five senses detect physical stimuli with incredibly sensitive and specialized organs. The information these organs gather is transformed into nerve impulses and directed toward the central nervous system, where it is processed to give us a conscious representation of our environment.

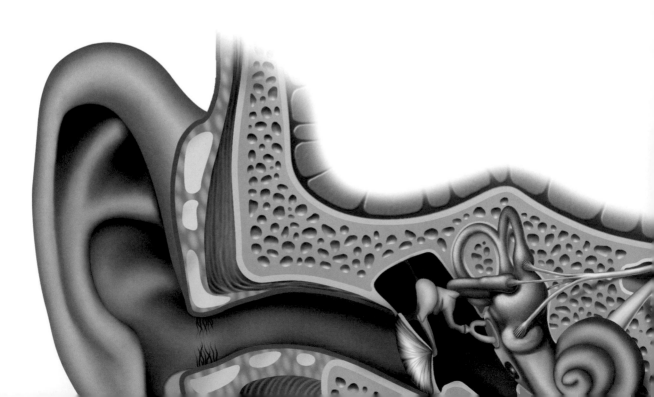

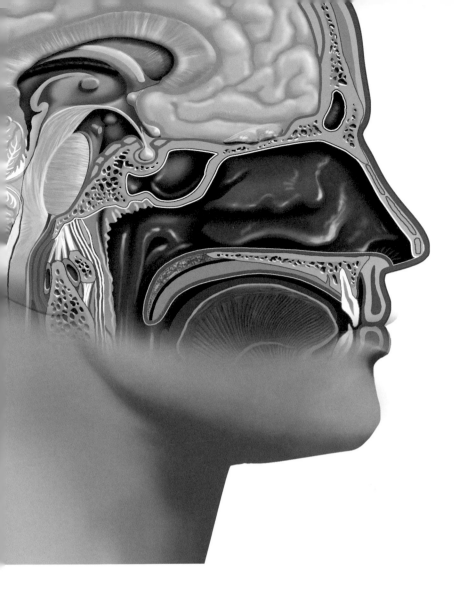

The Five Senses

Touch

Even though the sensation of pain is not pleasant, it plays a vital role in human life. Pain draws the attention of the central nervous system to cuts, burns, and punctures, as well as all other thermal and chemical assaults on the body. Without this alarm system, we would be at risk of not noticing when our bodies are under attack and being damaged.

When the skin's specialized receptors detect something touching the body, they convert this information into nerve impulses that travel to the cerebrum through different nerve bundles. It is up to the central nervous system to process the message and respond appropriately.

TOUCH RECEPTORS

Receptors in the skin detect different types of stimuli that cause different types of sensations. Tactile sensations, such as light touch, vibration, and pressure, tell us about the weight, size, and consistency of the object touching the body; thermal sensations tell us about the object's temperature; and painful sensations are produced whenever the skin is injured. These stimuli are perceived by receptors located in the dermis and epidermis, most of which can only detect one or a few types of stimuli.

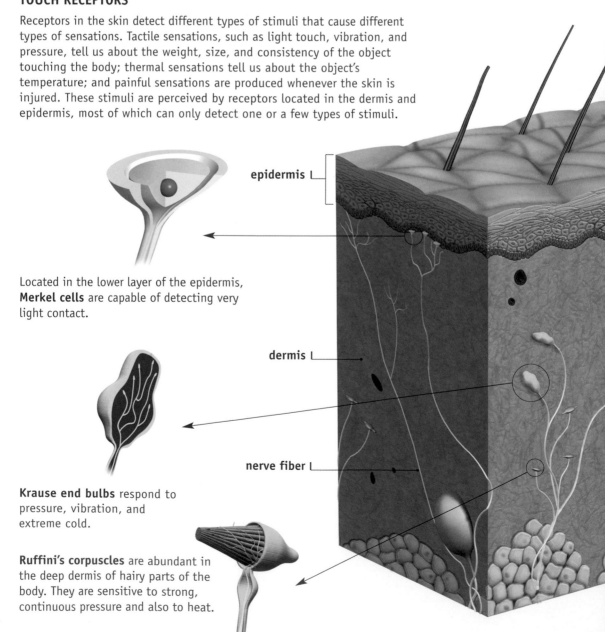

epidermis

dermis

nerve fiber

Located in the lower layer of the epidermis, **Merkel cells** are capable of detecting very light contact.

Krause end bulbs respond to pressure, vibration, and extreme cold.

Ruffini's corpuscles are abundant in the deep dermis of hairy parts of the body. They are sensitive to strong, continuous pressure and also to heat.

THE NERVE PATHS OF TOUCH

Sensory nerve impulses take one of two different paths to the cerebrum. Minute touch signals from Meissner's corpuscles travel to the brain stem directly and, thus, reach the somatosensory cortex very rapidly—within a few hundredths of a second.

On the other hand, both pain signals sent by free nerve endings and diffuse touch signals sent by Pacinian corpuscles travel through the spinothalamic tracts; they are analyzed in the gray matter of the spinal cord, which modulates and integrates them before sending them to the cerebrum. Their transmission time is therefore longer; one second passes between occurrence of a stimulus and its reception by the cortex.

The **somatosensory cortex**, located in the parietal lobe of the brain, is where tactile sensations become conscious. There, a mental representation of the region touched and the type of contact forms. This mental image is then compared and integrated with previous sensations, such as those detected by the visual and auditory systems.

Nerve bundles converge in the **thalamus**, which leads to the somatosensory cortex.

Free nerve endings, which are abundant at the surface of the dermis, are nociceptors, or cells that react to pain-causing stimuli.

brain stem

Meissner's corpuscles are cells that are sensitive to minute touches; they are located in the upper part of the dermis of the hands, feet, lips, and genital organs.

spinothalamic tract

Pacinian corpuscles are located in the deep dermis and react to vibrations and strong, continuous pressure.

nerve fiber

spinal cord

The Eye

An organic for capturing light

An organ for capturing light

Although it weighs just .25 ounce (7 grams) and has an average diameter of only .9 inch (24 millimeters), the human eye is a biological camera whose complexity and capacities surpass the most advanced humanmade optical equipment. Our highly evolved eyes include two lenses and a pupil that deflect a precise quantity of light rays toward the retina, where more than 130 million photoreceptors convert the light into neural signals that can be interpreted by the brain.

INSIDE THE EYEBALL

The eye, which is recessed within a bony socket, is a hollow body filled with a gelatinous substance called the vitreous body. It is covered with several layers of tunics—the retina, the choroid, and the sclera—that form the coat of the eyeball. The sclera covers the whole eyeball except for the perfectly transparent section at its front, known as the cornea.

Light enters the eye through the cornea ❶, which is the principal ocular lens. It then travels through the opening called the pupil ❷. Behind the pupil is the crystalline lens ❸, which converges light rays toward the retina ❹.

The **choroid** is the vascular layer located between the sclera and the retina. It supplies the retina with nutrients and oxygen.

The whitish **sclera** is the thickest layer of the coat of the eyeball. It is covered with a mucous layer known as the conjunctiva, and it protects the fragile internal structures of the eye.

vitreous body

Via suspensory ligaments called zonules, the **muscles of the ciliary body** pull or release the lens to change its curvature.

Its curved shape enables the **cornea** to deflect light at a sharp angle toward the interior of the eye.

The **pupil** changes size in order to adapt to the quantity of light rays that reach it.

The **crystalline lens** has two convex curvatures.

The **iris** is the muscle that dilates or contracts to determine the size of the pupil. Its color varies from individual to individual.

The eyeball has six **extraocular muscles** that move it in different directions.

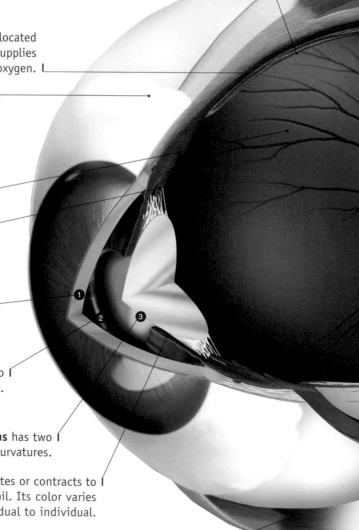

retina

THE ROLE OF THE RETINA

Light rays ❺ that reach the retina pass through several layers of cells before reaching its photoreceptor cells ❻, which are the only cells that have the pigments capable of transforming light into electrical impulses. These impulses are transmitted by intermediary neurons ❼ to the optic nerve ❽. The optic nerve, in turn, carries the impulses to the brain.

The retina contains two types of photoreceptor cells: cones and rods. There are around 125 million rods but only 6 million cones. Although rods do not detect colors, they are very sensitive to contrasts in light. Cones, on the other hand, are specialized for detecting colors.

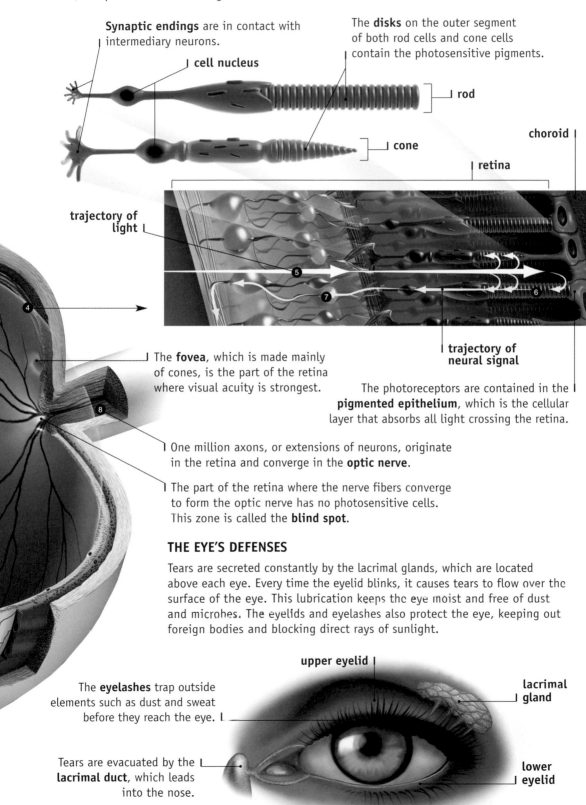

Synaptic endings are in contact with intermediary neurons.

cell nucleus

The **disks** on the outer segment of both rod cells and cone cells contain the photosensitive pigments.

rod

cone

choroid

retina

trajectory of light

trajectory of neural signal

The **fovea**, which is made mainly of cones, is the part of the retina where visual acuity is strongest.

The photoreceptors are contained in the **pigmented epithelium**, which is the cellular layer that absorbs all light crossing the retina.

One million axons, or extensions of neurons, originate in the retina and converge in the **optic nerve**.

The part of the retina where the nerve fibers converge to form the optic nerve has no photosensitive cells. This zone is called the **blind spot**.

THE EYE'S DEFENSES

Tears are secreted constantly by the lacrimal glands, which are located above each eye. Every time the eyelid blinks, it causes tears to flow over the surface of the eye. This lubrication keeps the eye moist and free of dust and microbes. The eyelids and eyelashes also protect the eye, keeping out foreign bodies and blocking direct rays of sunlight.

upper eyelid

The **eyelashes** trap outside elements such as dust and sweat before they reach the eye.

Tears are evacuated by the **lacrimal duct**, which leads into the nose.

lacrimal gland

lower eyelid

Sight

Our most highly developed sense

Human beings have remarkable visual acuity; our sense of sight, in fact, is vastly superior to our other senses. The perception of shapes, distances, colors, and movements in our environment is a complex process that uses a chain of optical and nervous components, from the eye's cornea to the brain's cortex.

HOW THE EYE FOCUSES

Light rays emanating from objects we look at are first deflected by the cornea to the crystalline lens. Unlike the curve of the cornea, the curve of the crystalline lens is variable, causing the images of objects at different distances to converge on the retina. The precision needed in this optical system, however, makes it particularly fragile; the slightest imperfection in the shape of the eyeball or the curve of the cornea leads to an imbalance for which the crystalline lens cannot always compensate. In these cases, the image is not focused on the retina but either in front of it or behind it. This problem makes vision blurry.

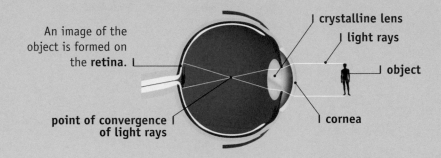

An image of the object is formed on the **retina**.

crystalline lens

light rays

object

point of convergence of light rays

cornea

Myopia is a defect in which the image of a distant object is formed in front of the retina. This problem is corrected with a concave lens, which pushes the point of convergence of light rays farther back in the eye.

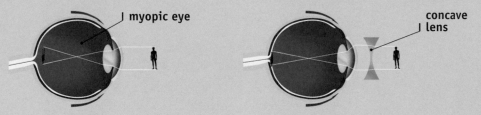

myopic eye

concave lens

Hyperopia, in contrast, is the defect in which the image is formed behind the retina. To correct this problem, a convex lens is used to bring the point of convergence forward in the eye.

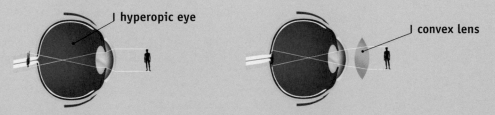

hyperopic eye

convex lens

Astigmatism is a defect in the curve of the cornea or the crystalline lens preventing homogeneous convergence of light rays. An asymmetrical lens can correct this problem.

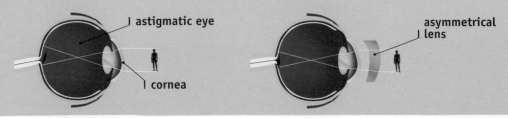

astigmatic eye

asymmetrical lens

cornea

SIGHT: FROM THE CORNEA TO THE CORTEX

When an object ❶ enters our field of vision, each of our two eyes perceives it from a slightly different angle. This slight difference enables us to evaluate its distance and see its shape in three dimensions. Light rays are deflected as they pass through the cornea and the crystalline lens ❷ in such a way that the object is inverted as it reaches the retina ❸. The optical image is then converted by photoreceptor cells in the retina into electrical impulses that reach the optic nerves ❹. The two optic nerves meet in the optic chiasma ❺, which leads to outgrowths of the thalamus called the lateral geniculate bodies ❻. The information is then transmitted by optic radiation to the visual cortex ❼, where the image is reconstructed right side up ❽.

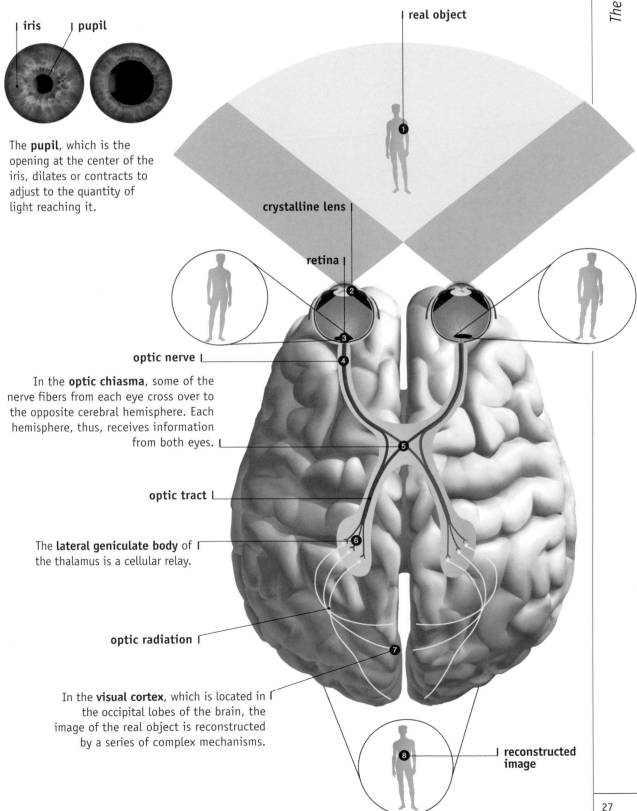

iris | pupil

The **pupil**, which is the opening at the center of the iris, dilates or contracts to adjust to the quantity of light reaching it.

real object

crystalline lens

retina

optic nerve

In the **optic chiasma**, some of the nerve fibers from each eye cross over to the opposite cerebral hemisphere. Each hemisphere, thus, receives information from both eyes.

optic tract

The **lateral geniculate body** of the thalamus is a cellular relay.

optic radiation

In the **visual cortex**, which is located in the occipital lobes of the brain, the image of the real object is reconstructed by a series of complex mechanisms.

reconstructed image

The Ear

The Five Senses

From the delicate tinkling of a needle bouncing on a glass table to the deafening roar of a plane taking off, our ears enable us to distinguish almost 400,000 sounds. There is more to our ears than just their visible, external parts; two groups of small, fragile internal structures housed in bony cavities inside the head are essential for sensing sound.

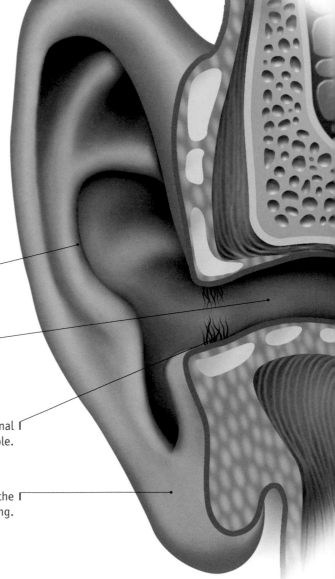

helix

THE THREE PARTS OF THE EAR

Our auditory system has three parts. The outer ear captures sound vibrations and directs them to the auditory canal. The middle ear, which is bounded by a fine membrane called the tympanum or tympanic membrane, contains the hammer, the anvil, and the stirrup, a group of three tiny bones, only a few millimeters long each. This chamber is connected to the nose and throat by a narrow passage known as the eustachian tube. Finally, the inner ear contains the liquid-filled spiral known as the cochlea, the cochlear nerve, and other minute organs.

The **auricle** has many cartilaginous and cutaneous folds that capture sounds; it is the main part of the outer ear.

The **external auditory canal** is lined with hairs and covered with cerumen, or earwax, a substance that traps dust.

The **hairs** of the auditory canal play a protective role.

The **earlobe**, the fleshy extension of the auricle, is not involved in hearing.

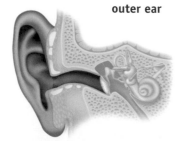

outer ear

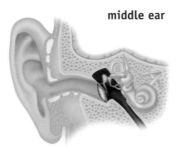

middle ear

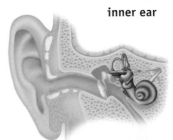

inner ear

THE AUDITORY CORTEX

Auditory messages are relayed by the auditory nerve to the auditory cortex, a zone of the cerebral cortex that itself has two areas. Specific sounds are identified in the primary auditory cortex. The secondary auditory cortex, which surrounds the primary audio cortex, provides a more diffuse representation of perceived sounds. These areas are next to Wernicke's area, which is a zone of the brain involved in language comprehension.

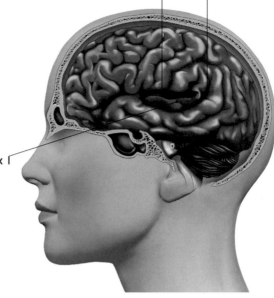

Wernicke's area

primary auditory cortex

secondary auditory cortex

tympanum

The three **semicircular canals** of the inner ear are the organs responsible for balance.

vestibule

The **vestibular nerve** transmits messages related to balance.

The cochlear nerve and the vestibular nerve join in the **inner auditory canal.**

The **cochlear nerve** carries the nerve signals of hearing.

round window

temporal bone

The **eustachian tube** enables pressure on either side of the tympanum to be equalized.

A cavity of the temporal bone houses the liquid-filled **cochlea**. This part of the inner ear consists of a system of membranous and bony partitions that define three canals that spiral around a central axis. One of these canals contains the organ of Corti. Since the organ of Corti is linked to the cochlear nerve, it is the true organ of hearing.

hammer (malleus)

anvil (incus)

stirrup (stapes)

The **ossicles** of the middle ear—the hammer, the anvil, and the stirrup—are the smallest bones in the human body. The stirrup is only around .2 inch (4 mm) long.

Perception of Sound
The path of vibrations through the ear

Our auditory system functions like a complex trap that routes sound vibrations through air in the outer ear, then through a solid in the middle ear, and, finally, through the liquid of the inner ear. Only at the end of this series of transmissions does the organ of Corti—the real auditory receptor—detect the frequency and intensity of sounds.

FROM THE TYMPANUM TO THE COCHLEA

Sound, when directed from the auricle through the external auditory canal, makes the tympanum vibrate ❶. The ossicles ❷, located behind the tympanum, amplify this vibration and transmit it to the entrance of the inner ear, known as the oval window ❸. The sound vibration then travels through the scala vestibuli of the cochlea ❹ and stimulates the organ of Corti. High-frequency sounds are felt at the base of the cochlea's spiral, while low-frequency sounds are felt at its apex. When the vibrations arrive at the helicotrema ❺, they travel up the scala tympani and leave the cochlea through the round window ❻.

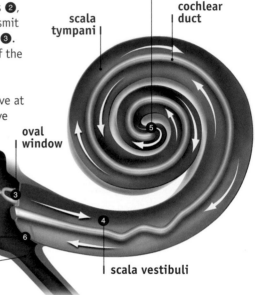

helicotrema

cochlear duct

scala tympani

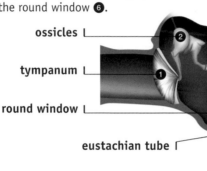

ossicles

tympanum

round window

eustachian tube

oval window

scala vestibuli

INSIDE THE COCHLEA

The cochlea is composed of three parallel spiral-shaped canals filled with liquid. The cochlear duct is bounded by membranes that separate it completely from the scala vestibuli and scala tympani. These canals are connected by a passage called the helicotrema, which is located at the top of the cochlea.

Sound waves travel through the scala vestibuli and cause the basilar membrane, which sits against the organ of Corti, to vibrate. The ciliated cells in the organ of Corti transform the vibrations into nerve impulses, which are transmitted to the cerebrum by the cochlear nerve. The sound waves leave the cochlea through the scala tympani.

scala vestibuli

cochlear nerve

scala tympani

cochlear duct

organ of Corti

scala tympani

The stiffness of the **basilar membrane** varies from the base of the cochlea to its apex.

Located between the basilar and tectorial membranes of the cochlea, the **hair cells of the organ of Corti** react to the slightest vibrations by generating nerve impulses.

scala vestibuli

tectorial membrane

vestibular membrane

cochlear duct

Balance

A sixth sense?

Our five senses inform us about our environment, but they do not tell us everything about the position of our body in relation to the space around us. Having information about our body in space, however, is important in order for us to keep our balance and move effectively. The organ responsible for this "sixth sense" is located in the inner ear, where it sits beside the auditory organ.

DYNAMIC BALANCE

Three semicircular canals, corresponding to the three dimensions of space, evaluate the position of the head when it is moving. Each of the canals, which are filled with endolymph, ends in an ampulla. This swelling contains hair cells whose cilia are enveloped in a cone-shaped gelatinous mass called a cupula.

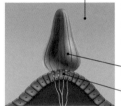

| endolymph

When the head is still, the cupula does not move.

| cupula

| hair cell

When the head moves, the endolymph in the cupula moves and stimulates the hair cells, which send nerve messages via the vestibular nerve.

If movement of the head stops suddenly, the endolymph continues to move for a few moments, causing an imbalance or dizziness.

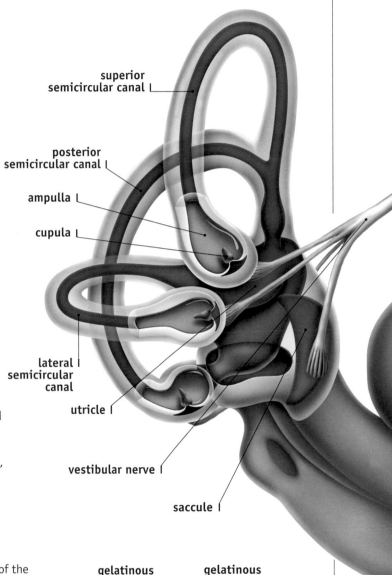

superior semicircular canal |

posterior semicircular canal |

ampulla |

cupula |

lateral semicircular canal |

utricle |

vestibular nerve |

saccule |

STATIC BALANCE

Static balance, or the evaluation of the position of the head in relation to the ground, is obtained using hair cells in the utricle and the saccule, which are the two membranous pockets in the inner ear. The cilia of the hair cells ❶ are immersed in a gelatinous mass that contains small particles called otoliths. When the head tilts, the otoliths are subjected to gravity, and they move the gelatinous mass ❷. As they tilt, the cilia modify the nerve impulses generated by the cells. This mechanism enables the body to detect variations as small as .5° in the tilt of the head.

gelatinous mass |

gelatinous mass |

otolith |

hair cell |

cilia |

nerve fiber |

Taste

A limited sense

Food lovers may find it hard to believe, but our ability to taste is limited to five basic flavors—sweet, salty, sour, bitter, and umami, or meaty—and it is not very sensitive. A chemical substance must be 25,000 times more concentrated to be perceived by taste receptors than by smell receptors.

What we call the flavor of a food is often a combination of smell and taste, perceived by both the olfactory receptors in the nasal cavity and the gustatory receptors in the tongue, palate, and oropharynx. Sensations of the consistency and temperature of food add to this combination of flavor sensations to inform us about the things we put in our mouths.

The **palatine tonsils**, which are located on either side of the posterior base of the tongue, contribute to immune-system defense by imprisoning bacteria that enter the body through air or food passages.

The **palatoglossal arch** is a muscular fold that links the tongue to the palate.

WHAT DOES SALIVA DO?

Sapid substances, or substances that produce a taste, must be in liquid form for the taste buds to react to them. Saliva dissolves substances and, thus, allows taste to be perceived. This liquid is produced by three pairs of major **salivary glands**—the left and right parotids, sublinguals, and submandibulars—and by numerous minor salivary glands located in the mucosae of the oral cavity. Salivary glands are controlled by sympathetic and parasympathetic nerves and function reflexively when stimulated by various receptors. Many visual, psychological, tactile, olfactory, and gustatory stimuli may cause a reflexive flow of saliva.

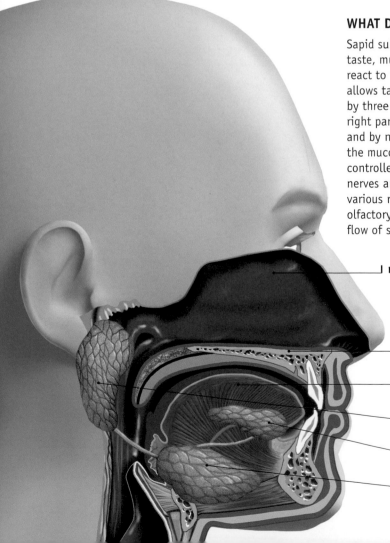

nasal cavity

The **palate** divides the mouth and the nasal cavities. It is made of the bony part in the front called the vault, or hard palate, and the musculo-membranous part in the back called the velum, or soft palate.

tongue

parotid gland

sublingual gland

submandibular gland

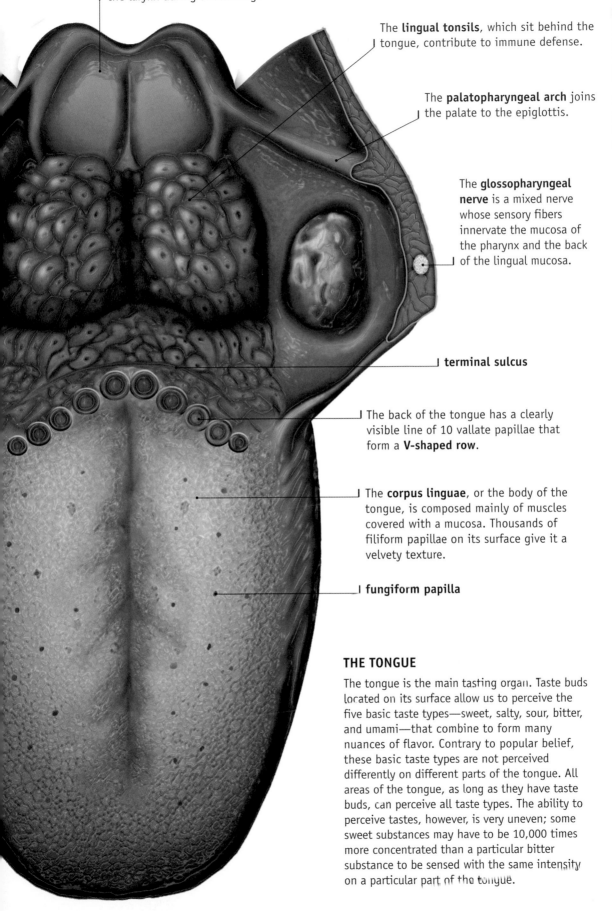

The **epiglottis** is a cartilaginous flap that closes the entrance to the larynx during swallowing.

The **lingual tonsils**, which sit behind the tongue, contribute to immune defense.

The **palatopharyngeal arch** joins the palate to the epiglottis.

The **glossopharyngeal nerve** is a mixed nerve whose sensory fibers innervate the mucosa of the pharynx and the back of the lingual mucosa.

terminal sulcus

The back of the tongue has a clearly visible line of 10 vallate papillae that form a **V-shaped row.**

The **corpus linguae**, or the body of the tongue, is composed mainly of muscles covered with a mucosa. Thousands of filiform papillae on its surface give it a velvety texture.

fungiform papilla

THE TONGUE

The tongue is the main tasting organ. Taste buds located on its surface allow us to perceive the five basic taste types—sweet, salty, sour, bitter, and umami—that combine to form many nuances of flavor. Contrary to popular belief, these basic taste types are not perceived differently on different parts of the tongue. All areas of the tongue, as long as they have taste buds, can perceive all taste types. The ability to perceive tastes, however, is very uneven; some sweet substances may have to be 10,000 times more concentrated than a particular bitter substance to be sensed with the same intensity on a particular part of the tongue.

Taste Receptors

The sense of taste uses a very large number of receptors that are housed in the folds of the lingual papillae. Each individual has between 200,000 and 500,000 taste-receptor cells spread over the top of the tongue, in the throat, on the insides of the cheeks, on the back part of the palate, and on the epiglottis. These cells are constantly being replaced, since they only last about 10 days. With age, taste-receptor cells regenerate more slowly, causing a diminution in the sense of taste.

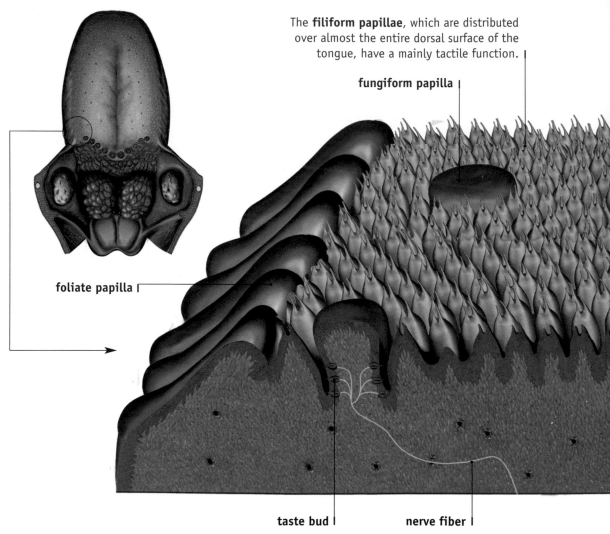

The **filiform papillae**, which are distributed over almost the entire dorsal surface of the tongue, have a mainly tactile function.

fungiform papilla

foliate papilla

taste bud

nerve fiber

THE LINGUAL PAPILLAE

The top of the tongue has a bumpy surface because it is covered with protuberances called lingual papillae. These irregular projections have a number of different shapes, though they are difficult to differentiate with the naked eye. The four main types of lingual papillae are filiform, fungiform, vallate, and foliate. Each type is located located at a different site on the tongue.

The vallate papillae, which are the largest of the lingual papillae, form a wide V-shape at the back of the tongue, with a groove on either side. Smaller but more numerous are the fungiform papillae, which look like small red balls scattered on the top of the tongue. The filiform papillae, which are conical in shape and have a ridge at their top, are spread over the entire surface of the tongue. Finally, the foliate papillae are found on either side of the top of the tongue, where they form series of parallel grooves. The taste buds are most numerous in the folds of the vallate papillae; there are far fewer of them among the fungiform papillae.

THE TASTE BUDS

The epithelium, or the top cellular layer, of the tongue, with its vallate and fungiform papillae, has many gustatory cells. Grouped into small buds with a maximum diameter of .002 inch (.05 mm), these cells have cilia called microvilli at their tips, which protrude from the epithelium and are covered in saliva. When the terminal ends of the microvilli come into contact with molecules corresponding to one of the four basic taste types, a cascade of biochemical reactions takes place. The gustatory cells then generate a nerve message that is transmitted to the cerebral cortex where it is interpreted as a taste sensation.

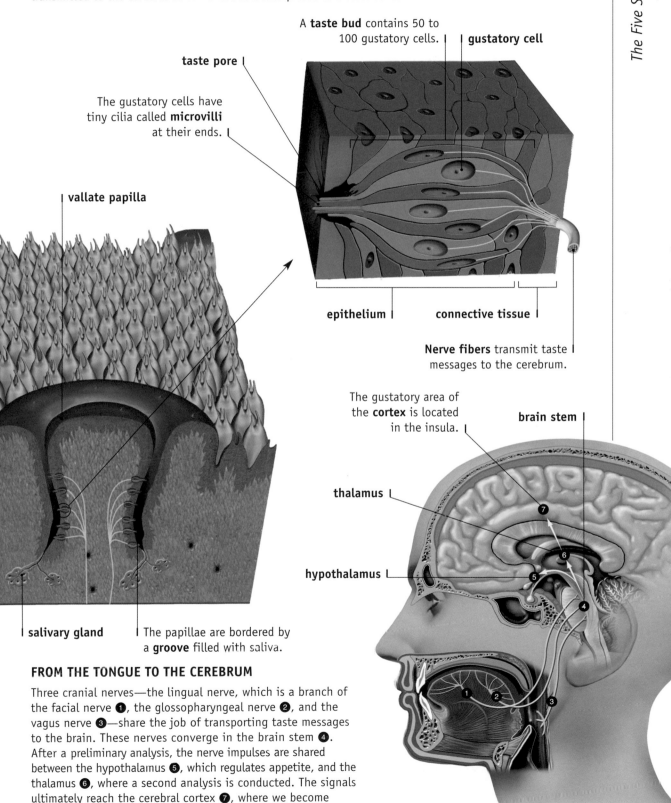

A **taste bud** contains 50 to 100 gustatory cells.

gustatory cell

taste pore

The gustatory cells have tiny cilia called **microvilli** at their ends.

vallate papilla

epithelium

connective tissue

Nerve fibers transmit taste messages to the cerebrum.

The gustatory area of the **cortex** is located in the insula.

brain stem

thalamus

hypothalamus

salivary gland

The papillae are bordered by a **groove** filled with saliva.

FROM THE TONGUE TO THE CEREBRUM

Three cranial nerves—the lingual nerve, which is a branch of the facial nerve ❶, the glossopharyngeal nerve ❷, and the vagus nerve ❸—share the job of transporting taste messages to the brain. These nerves converge in the brain stem ❹. After a preliminary analysis, the nerve impulses are shared between the hypothalamus ❺, which regulates appetite, and the thalamus ❻, where a second analysis is conducted. The signals ultimately reach the cerebral cortex ❼, where we become conscious of tastes and flavors.

Smell

Smell is perhaps the most mysterious sense. Its mechanisms are not yet completely understood, and its receptors are hidden within the nose. The olfactory epithelium, which is the cellular layer responsible for detection of odors, covers an area of .8 to 1.5 square inches (5 to 10 square centimeters) of our nasal cavity, and it contains from 10 million to 100 million smell receptors.

Although the human sense of smell is not as highly developed as that of other animals, an adult human is able to distinguish more than 10,000 different odors. This sensitivity, which helps us defend ourselves against dangers— for example, fire and natural gas poisoning—also enables us to better appreciate the flavors of the foods we eat.

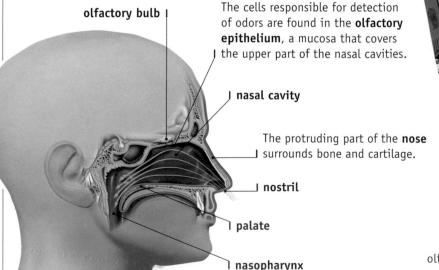

gland of Bowman

Mucus produced by the glands of Bowman humidifies the tiny cilia at the tips of the olfactory cells and dissolves odoriferous molecules to facilitate chemical reactions.

THE NASAL CAVITIES

The nasal cavities, which are open to the outside environment via the two nostrils, are the main entrance into the respiratory system. During respiration, odoriferous molecules contained in inhaled air activate the olfactory receptors in the two nasal cavities. These cavities are separated from the mouth by the palate but connected to it by the nasopharynx; odors from foods reach the olfactory epithelium through the nasopharynx.

olfactory bulb

The cells responsible for detection of odors are found in the **olfactory epithelium**, a mucosa that covers the upper part of the nasal cavities.

nasal cavity

The protruding part of the **nose** surrounds bone and cartilage.

nostril

palate

nasopharynx

The **supporting cells** that form the bulk of the olfactory epithelium do not have a sensory function.

THE NERVE PATHS FOR SMELL

From the olfactory bulbs ❶, nerve impulses travel to the limbic system of the cerebrum, where they come into contact with the areas of the the brain associated with emotions and memory, such as the mamillary bodies ❷. The existence of this pathway explains why a simple odor can instantly trigger very strong emotional reactions and provoke memories. Another part of the olfactory nerve travels through the thalamus ❸ to the orbitofrontal cortex ❹, where a conscious sensation of the odor is created.

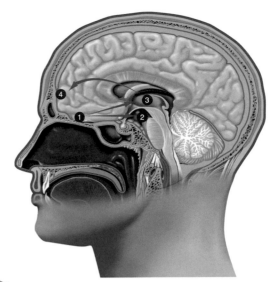

olfactory bulb

Mitral cells relay nerve impulses to the cerebrum.

ethmoid bone

connective tissue

The **axons** of the olfactory cells are grouped in bundles that cross the ethmoid bone.

Basal cells constantly produce new olfactory cells.

olfactory epithelium

olfactory cell

The mechanism that converts a chemical stimulus into a nerve impulse is located on the surface of the **olfactory cilia**.

mucous layer

odoriferous molecule

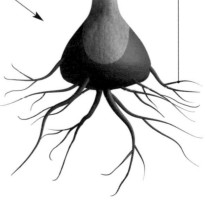

THE SMELL RECEPTORS

The olfactory cells are sensory neurons whose axons cross the ethmoid bone and enter the olfactory bulb, where, at one end, they form synaptic connections with interneurons called mitral cells. At their other end are dendrites, each with a dozen sensory hairs. Olfactory cells are unique among neurons in that they regenerate; regeneration occurs for no other neurons. The life span of olfactory neurons is about two months.

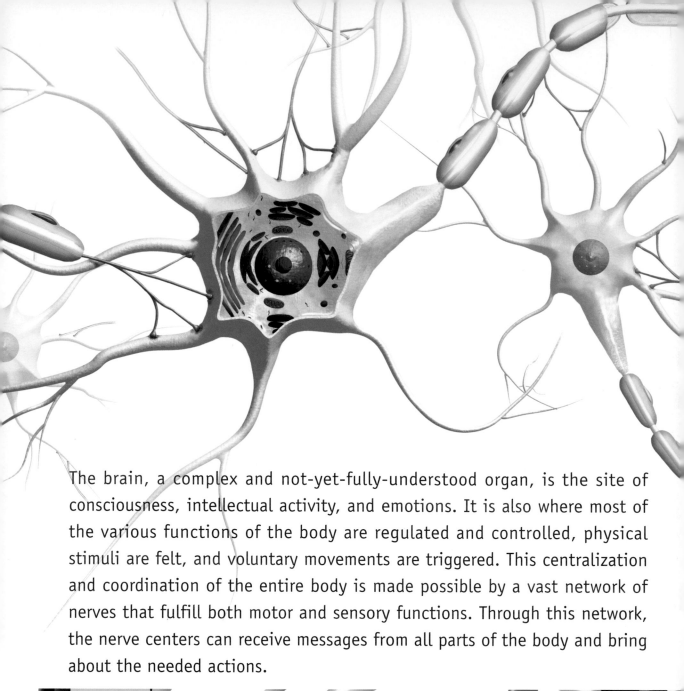

The brain, a complex and not-yet-fully-understood organ, is the site of consciousness, intellectual activity, and emotions. It is also where most of the various functions of the body are regulated and controlled, physical stimuli are felt, and voluntary movements are triggered. This centralization and coordination of the entire body is made possible by a vast network of nerves that fulfill both motor and sensory functions. Through this network, the nerve centers can receive messages from all parts of the body and bring about the needed actions.

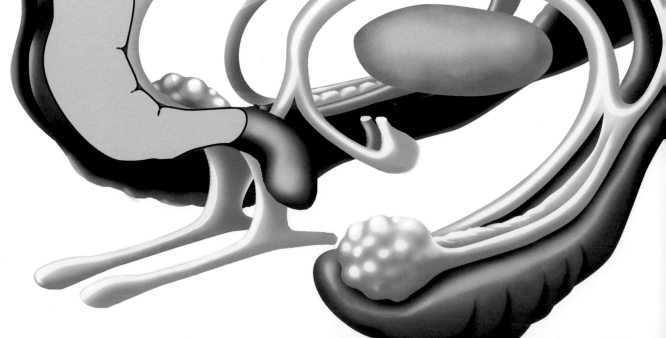

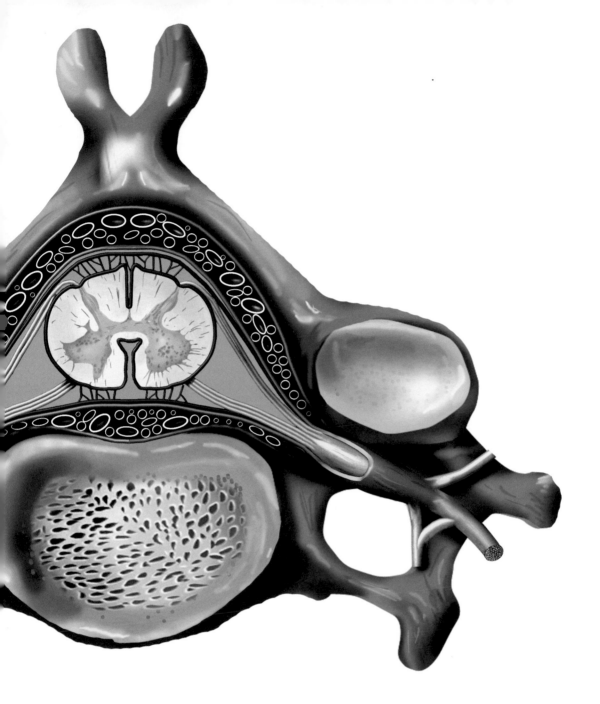

The Nervous System

Neurons

Cells that transmit nerve impulses

The nervous system is made up of cells called neurons. These highly specialized cells are unique in that they can carry electrical signals and transmit them to other nervous cells, muscular cells, and glandular cells. Every motor, sensory, and associative neuron consists of a cell body, which contains its nucleus; dendrites, which receive electrical impulses; and axons, which transmit these impulses.

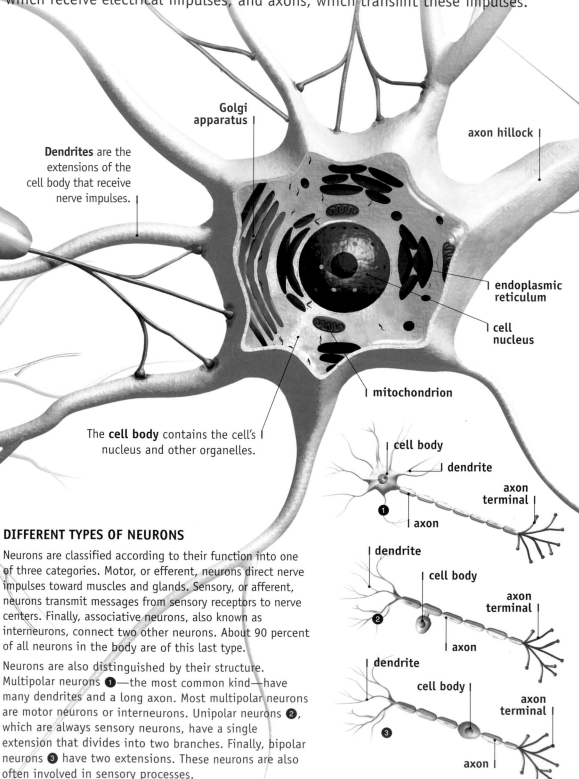

Golgi apparatus

axon hillock

Dendrites are the extensions of the cell body that receive nerve impulses.

endoplasmic reticulum

cell nucleus

mitochondrion

The **cell body** contains the cell's nucleus and other organelles.

cell body

dendrite

axon terminal

❶

axon

dendrite

cell body

axon terminal

❷

axon

dendrite

cell body

axon terminal

❸

axon

DIFFERENT TYPES OF NEURONS

Neurons are classified according to their function into one of three categories. Motor, or efferent, neurons direct nerve impulses toward muscles and glands. Sensory, or afferent, neurons transmit messages from sensory receptors to nerve centers. Finally, associative neurons, also known as interneurons, connect two other neurons. About 90 percent of all neurons in the body are of this last type.

Neurons are also distinguished by their structure. Multipolar neurons ❶—the most common kind—have many dendrites and a long axon. Most multipolar neurons are motor neurons or interneurons. Unipolar neurons ❷, which are always sensory neurons, have a single extension that divides into two branches. Finally, bipolar neurons ❸ have two extensions. These neurons are also often involved in sensory processes.

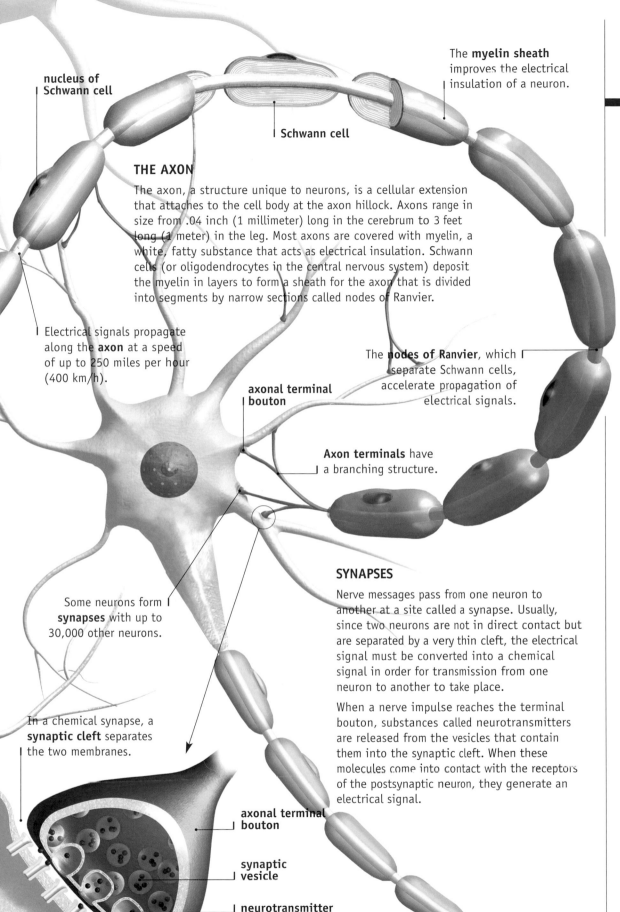

nucleus of Schwann cell

The **myelin sheath** improves the electrical insulation of a neuron.

Schwann cell

THE AXON

The axon, a structure unique to neurons, is a cellular extension that attaches to the cell body at the axon hillock. Axons range in size from .04 inch (1 millimeter) long in the cerebrum to 3 feet long (1 meter) in the leg. Most axons are covered with myelin, a white, fatty substance that acts as electrical insulation. Schwann cells (or oligodendrocytes in the central nervous system) deposit the myelin in layers to form a sheath for the axon that is divided into segments by narrow sections called nodes of Ranvier.

Electrical signals propagate along the **axon** at a speed of up to 250 miles per hour (400 km/h).

The **nodes of Ranvier**, which separate Schwann cells, accelerate propagation of electrical signals.

axonal terminal bouton

Axon terminals have a branching structure.

Some neurons form **synapses** with up to 30,000 other neurons.

SYNAPSES

Nerve messages pass from one neuron to another at a site called a synapse. Usually, since two neurons are not in direct contact but are separated by a very thin cleft, the electrical signal must be converted into a chemical signal in order for transmission from one neuron to another to take place.

When a nerve impulse reaches the terminal bouton, substances called neurotransmitters are released from the vesicles that contain them into the synaptic cleft. When these molecules come into contact with the receptors of the postsynaptic neuron, they generate an electrical signal.

In a chemical synapse, a **synaptic cleft** separates the two membranes.

axonal terminal bouton

synaptic vesicle

neurotransmitter

neurotransmitter receptor

postsynaptic neuron

The Central Nervous System
The control center for the nerve network

The nervous system is the network that allows for communication between the parts of the body and responses to all kinds of stimuli. It is responsible for the processing of sensory messages from the entire body and some of the actions of our organs and muscles, as well as for our intellectual activities. These many functions are made possible by coordination between the system of nerves that run throughout the body, called the peripheral nervous system—and the central nervous system.

Weighing between 2.8 and 3 pounds (1.3 and 1.4 kg), the **cerebrum** is the most highly developed part of the central nervous system.

The **cerebellum** is involved mainly in motor coordination, maintenance of balance, muscle tone, and posture.

THE CENTRAL NERVOUS SYSTEM

The central nervous system is composed of the brain—which consists of the cerebrum, the cerebellum, and the brain stem—and the spinal cord. Consisting of more than 100 billion neurons, the central nervous system is the command, control, and processing center for the body's nerve information.

The main task of the **brain stem** is to transmit messages between the spinal cord, the cerebrum, and the cerebellum.

Housed in the bony canal formed by the spine, the **spinal cord** extends from the brain stem to the second lumbar vertebra. The diameter of the spinal cord averages .8 inch (2 cm), but it is not uniform; the cord has two swellings, one in cervical region and the other lumbar in the lumbar region.

second lumbar vertebra

Below the second lumbar vertebra, the spinal cord is extended by the **filum terminale**, a long filament of connective tissue.

Each **spinal nerve** is attached to the spinal cord by a sensory root, in the back, and a motor root, in the front.

On each side of the spinal cord, a chain of **sympathetic ganglions** controls the contraction of visceral muscles.

GRAY MATTER AND WHITE MATTER

The spinal cord is composed of two types of substances. Gray matter, which forms an H shape in the center of the cord, consists of neuron cell bodies. The dorsal horns of the spinal cord's H-shaped gray matter contain the sensory neurons of the spinal nerves, while the ventral horns of the H-shape contain motor neurons.

The spinal cord's gray matter is surrounded by white matter, which consists of bundles of ascending and descending nerve fibers, or extensions of neurons. The ascending bundles of nerve fibers bring sensory information received by the dorsal horns to the brain, while the descending bundles transmit motor impulses to the ventral horns of the spinal cord.

THE SPINAL CORD

The spinal cord provides a link between the brain and the 30 pairs of spinal nerves that are attached to it by their sensory and motor roots. Made of soft, fragile tissue, the spinal cord is protected by various membranes and liquids within the spinal canal, which is formed by the vertebrae of the spine.

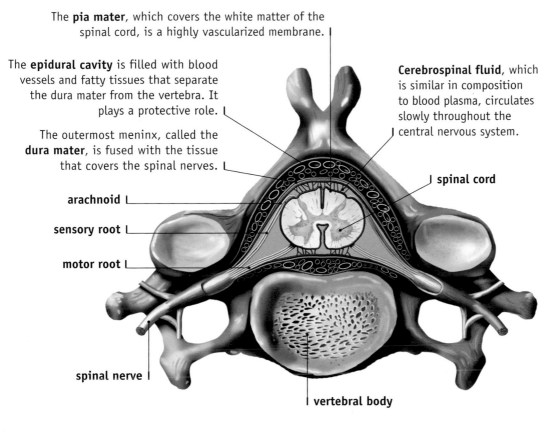

The **pia mater**, which covers the white matter of the spinal cord, is a highly vascularized membrane.

The **epidural cavity** is filled with blood vessels and fatty tissues that separate the dura mater from the vertebra. It plays a protective role.

The outermost meninx, called the **dura mater**, is fused with the tissue that covers the spinal nerves.

arachnoid

sensory root

motor root

spinal nerve

Cerebrospinal fluid, which is similar in composition to blood plasma, circulates slowly throughout the central nervous system.

spinal cord

vertebral body

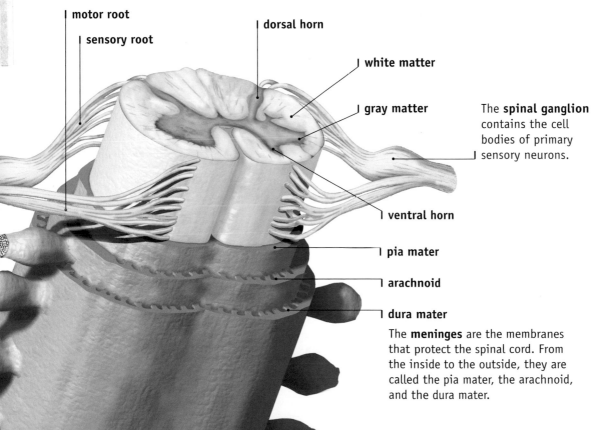

motor root

sensory root

dorsal horn

white matter

gray matter

The **spinal ganglion** contains the cell bodies of primary sensory neurons.

ventral horn

pia mater

arachnoid

dura mater

The **meninges** are the membranes that protect the spinal cord. From the inside to the outside, they are called the pia mater, the arachnoid, and the dura mater.

The Brain

The core of the nervous system

The brain is the central component of the nervous system. This organ consists of the brain stem, the cerebellum, and the cerebrum; the cerebrum makes up almost 90 percent of its volume. Housed in the skull, the brain communicates with the rest of the body via the cranial nerves and the spinal cord.

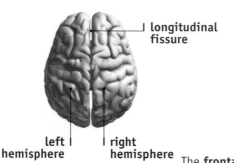

longitudinal fissure

left hemisphere

right hemisphere

THE SHAPE OF THE BRAIN

The cerebrum is a soft mass measuring about 85 cubic inches (1,400 cubic centimeters) and divided into two hemispheres by a deep groove called the longitudinal fissure. Other fissures define zones known as lobes, while shallower grooves separate gyri, or convolutions, whose patterns vary from individual to individual. The cerebellum, located under the cerebrum and behind the brain stem, is also divided into two hemispheres.

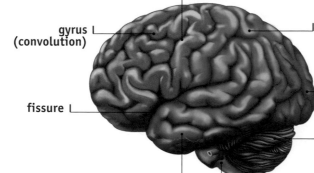

The **frontal lobe** is responsible for thought, language, emotions, and voluntary movements.

gyrus (convolution)

The **parietal lobe** is responsible for perception and interpretation of the sense of touch.

fissure

Visual images are processed in the **occipital lobe**.

cerebellum

The **temporal lobe** recognizes and interprets sounds and helps form new memories.

brain stem

The superior and inferior **colliculi** relay visual and auditory sensations throughout the cerebrum.

The **midbrain** consists of the four colliculi and the two cerebral peduncles.

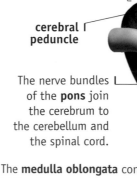

THE BRAIN STEM

The brain stem is the structure that connects the cerebrum and the spinal cord. It shares the basic tissue structure of white matter covering a core of gray matter with the spinal cord. Located deep in the heart of the cerebrum, the brain stem's three main parts—the medulla oblongata, the pons, and the midbrain—contain ascending and descending nerve bundles that link the cerebrum and cerebellum to the rest of the body. Since 10 of the 12 pairs of cranial nerves are directly attached to the brain stem, this structure also plays an essential role in the innervation of the head.

cerebral peduncle

The nerve bundles of the **pons** join the cerebrum to the cerebellum and the spinal cord.

The **medulla oblongata** controls vital functions such as respiration, circulation, heart rhythm, coughing, and swallowing.

spinal cord

THE PROTECTION OF THE BRAIN

The three meninges—the dura mater, the arachnoid, and the pia mater—that surround the spinal cord also cover and protect the brain. These membranes are themselves covered by several successive protective envelopes: the galea aponeurotica, which is a layer of tendons; the bones of the skull; and the skin.

In addition to its protective coverings, the cerebral material sits in cerebrospinal fluid, which gives both chemical protection and cushioning to the brain. This fluid forms inside several cavities within the brain—the lateral ventricles, the third ventricle, and the fourth ventricle—and then circulates throughout the central nervous system, including in the subarachnoid space.

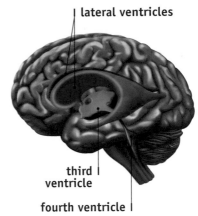

lateral ventricles

third ventricle

fourth ventricle

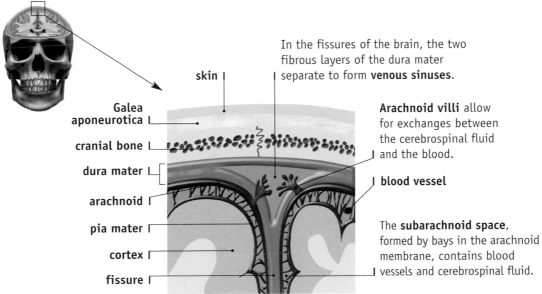

skin

In the fissures of the brain, the two fibrous layers of the dura mater separate to form **venous sinuses**.

Galea aponeurotica

cranial bone

dura mater

arachnoid

pia mater

cortex

fissure

Arachnoid villi allow for exchanges between the cerebrospinal fluid and the blood.

blood vessel

The **subarachnoid space**, formed by bays in the arachnoid membrane, contains blood vessels and cerebrospinal fluid.

THE CEREBELLUM

Located in the back of the brain, the cerebellum is separated from the occipital lobes by a fold in the meninges called the tentorium cerebelli. The hemispheres of the cerebellum, which are connected by a central projection known as the vermis, have a folded surface very different from that of the cerebrum.

The role of the cerebellum is to regulate and coordinate movements. To perform this function, the cerebellum continually analyzes messages sent by the sensory receptors and adjusts tension in the muscles by inhibiting commands issued by the motor area of the cerebrum. Because the cerebellum is linked to the organs of balance, it also regulates the posture of the body by controlling the involved muscles.

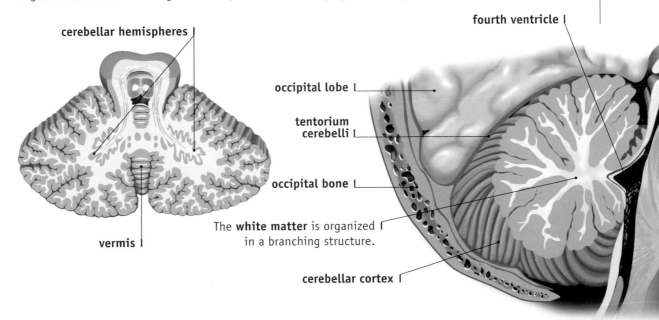

cerebellar hemispheres

fourth ventricle

occipital lobe

tentorium cerebelli

occipital bone

The **white matter** is organized in a branching structure.

vermis

cerebellar cortex

The Cerebrum

Extraordinary complexity

The human cerebrum bears traces of the different stages of animal evolution. Most of its vital basic functions, thus, are provided by components very deep within the cerebrum, such as the hypothalamus. Covering this "reptilian" part of the cerebrum is the limbic system, which controls more highly evolved cerebral functions such as memory, emotions, and learning. The cerebral cortex—the most recently developed zone—is the area that is involved in thought, language, voluntary movements, and conscious feeling of sensations.

INSIDE THE CEREBRUM

Like the spinal cord, the cerebrum is formed of gray matter and white matter. Gray matter, which is made up of neuron cell bodies, is found in the cerebral cortex and in certain central bodies such as the thalamus. White matter, which consists of nerve fibers, provides communication between the different parts of the central nervous system.

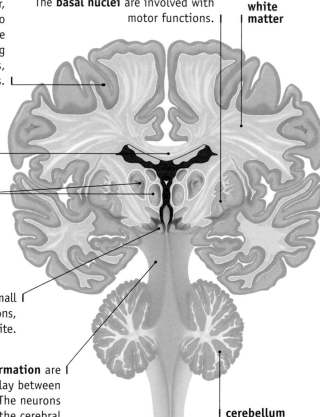

The **basal nuclei** are involved with motor functions.

white matter

The cerebrum is covered by a layer of gray matter, called the **cerebral cortex,** that is between .08 to .2 inch (2 and 5 mm) thick. This zone of the cerebrum plays a fundamental role in interpreting sensory messages, commanding voluntary actions, and carrying out intellectual functions.

The two cerebral hemispheres are linked by a group of commissures formed of white matter, the larger of which is called the **corpus callosum.**

Buried deep within the cerebrum, the **thalamus** consists of two masses located on either side of the brain's third ventricle. This structure is a relay between the sense organs and the sensory areas of the cerebral cortex.

The **hypothalamus** is made up of a number of small masses that control the body's vital functions, including body-heat regulation and appetite.

The many neurons of the **reticular formation** are interwoven with the brain stem, forming a relay between the sensory nerve bundles and the cerebrum. The neurons of this structure stimulate the activity of the cerebral cortex and maintain it in an alert state.

cerebellum

BRAIN WAVES

An electroencephalogram pictures the electrical activity, or brain waves, of the cerebrum as it can be detected when electrodes are attached to a person's scalp. The frequency and intensity of brain waves varies according to state of activity. During deep sleep, brain waves have high amplitude and low frequency; their frequency rises when the subject is awake but relaxed. During activity or dreaming, brain waves have higher frequencies but lower amplitudes.

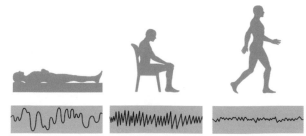

THE LIMBIC SYSTEM

The limbic system is superimposed on the primitive structures of the cerebrum, and it consists of certain parts of the basal nuclei, including the hypothalamus, parts of the thalamus, and interconnecting bundles of white matter. This system controls instinctive and emotional reactions—including fear, anger, and pleasure—and associates them with more evolved zones of the cerebral cortex, thus helping to produce complex behaviors. The limbic system is also where, through mechanisms that are not yet fully understood, memories are formed. The presence of olfactory bulbs in this region of the cerebrum also explains our emotional reactions to smells.

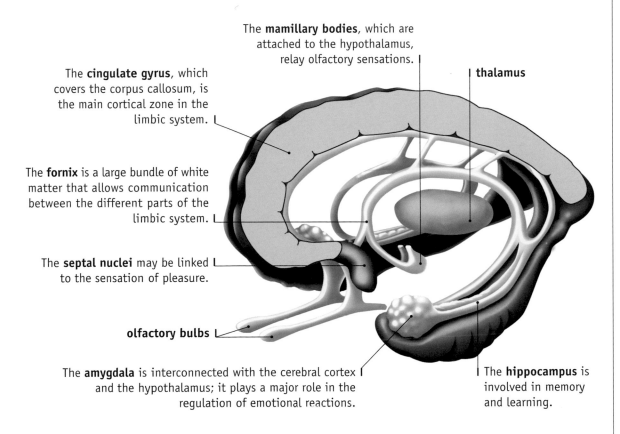

The **mamillary bodies**, which are attached to the hypothalamus, relay olfactory sensations.

thalamus

The **cingulate gyrus**, which covers the corpus callosum, is the main cortical zone in the limbic system.

The **fornix** is a large bundle of white matter that allows communication between the different parts of the limbic system.

The **septal nuclei** may be linked to the sensation of pleasure.

olfactory bulbs

The **amygdala** is interconnected with the cerebral cortex and the hypothalamus; it plays a major role in the regulation of emotional reactions.

The **hippocampus** is involved in memory and learning.

GROWTH OF THE CEREBRUM

In the embryo's first weeks of growth, it develops a primitive central nervous system. At 7 weeks ❶, three zones can already be identified: the forebrain, with the eye buds; the midbrain; and the hindbrain, where the cranial nerves are beginning to grow. At 11 weeks ❷, the hindbrain has divided into the cerebellum and the pons, while the forebrain has grown considerably. At birth ❸, the cerebrum is the largest part of the brain. By this time, gyri have formed on its surface.

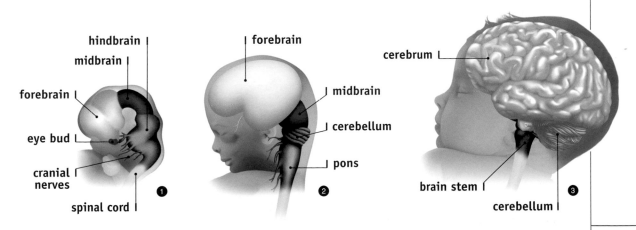

hindbrain
midbrain
forebrain
eye bud
cranial nerves
spinal cord
❶

forebrain
midbrain
cerebellum
pons
❷

cerebrum
brain stem
cerebellum
❸

The Peripheral Nervous System

A network of sensory and motor nerves

The central nervous system communicates with the rest of the body through 43 pairs of nerves—12 pairs of cranial nerves directly connected to the cerebrum and 31 pairs of spinal nerves linked to the spinal cord. This network, which constitutes the peripheral nervous system, or PNS, branches out to every part of the body.

There are two types of nerve impulses: sensory and motor. In the case of sensory nerve impulses, nerve terminals send messages to the central nervous system, or CNS. In the case of motor nerve impulses, the CNS commands a muscle to contract. Some nerves, called mixed nerves, perform both types of tasks.

CRANIAL NERVES

Twelve pairs of nerves—numbered I to XII—link directly to the cerebrum. These cranial nerves innervate mainly the head and neck. Some cranial nerves, such as the optic nerve, the auditory nerve, and the olfactory nerve, have strictly sensory functions, while others perform only motor tasks. Certain cranial nerves are mixed nerves, performing both sensory and motor tasks.

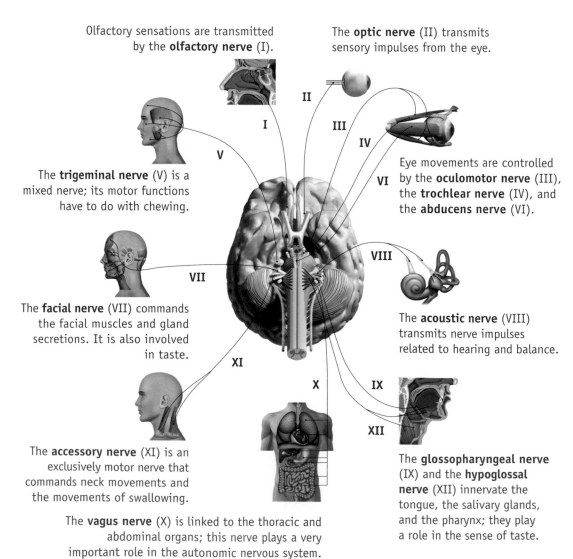

Olfactory sensations are transmitted by the **olfactory nerve** (I).

The **optic nerve** (II) transmits sensory impulses from the eye.

The **trigeminal nerve** (V) is a mixed nerve; its motor functions have to do with chewing.

Eye movements are controlled by the **oculomotor nerve** (III), the **trochlear nerve** (IV), and the **abducens nerve** (VI).

The **facial nerve** (VII) commands the facial muscles and gland secretions. It is also involved in taste.

The **acoustic nerve** (VIII) transmits nerve impulses related to hearing and balance.

The **accessory nerve** (XI) is an exclusively motor nerve that commands neck movements and the movements of swallowing.

The **glossopharyngeal nerve** (IX) and the **hypoglossal nerve** (XII) innervate the tongue, the salivary glands, and the pharynx; they play a role in the sense of taste.

The **vagus nerve** (X) is linked to the thoracic and abdominal organs; this nerve plays a very important role in the autonomic nervous system.

A sheath of connective tissue called the **perineurium** covers each bundle of neurons.

THE ANATOMY OF A NERVE

In the peripheral nervous system, the axons of neurons, which are generally covered with myelin, are grouped in bundles. Several bundles are, in turn, held together by an envelope of connective tissue, called epineurium, in order to form a nerve.

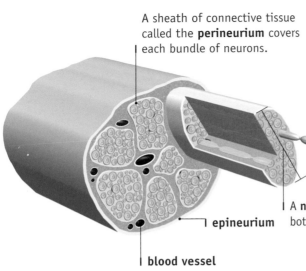

myelinated axon

epineurium

A **nerve-fiber bundle** may contain both sensory and motor neurons.

blood vessel

The **brachial plexus** branches into the radial, median, and ulnar nerves that innervate most of the arm.

THE SPINAL NERVES

The 62 spinal nerves, which are each linked to the spinal cord by a sensory root and a motor root, are all mixed nerves. They leave the spinal canal by narrow passages between the vertebrae called vertebral foramens, branch into ventral rami, rami communicantes, and dorsal rami, and then join together to form local networks called plexuses.

The 8 pairs of **cervical nerves** innervate the head, neck, shoulders, and upper limbs.

The ventral rami of the 12 pairs of **thoracic nerves** do not form plexuses. Because they are aligned between the ribs, they are called intercostal nerves.

radial nerve

median nerve

The 5 pairs of **lumbar nerves** serve mainly the abdomen and the front of the lower limbs.

ulnar nerve

The genital organs, buttocks, and most of the backs of the lower limbs are innervated by the 5 pairs of **sacral nerves**.

The two **coccygeal nerves** are relatively undeveloped.

The main branch of the sacral plexus is the **sciatic nerve**—the largest nerve in the body. Its branches, including the tibial nerve, the peroneal nerve, and the plantar nerves, innervate the back part of the lower limbs.

The front of the thigh is innervated by the **femoral nerve.**

peroneal nerve

tibial nerve

The internal and external **plantar nerves** innervate the bottom of the foot.

The Motor Functions of the Nervous System

How the body's muscles are activated

On one hand, the smooth muscles that contract and relax the internal organs are commanded by the autonomic nervous system, which is controlled mainly by the brain stem. On the other hand, the human body's skeletal muscles allow it to perform a wide variety of very specific movements. The motor cortex, an area of the cerebrum located behind the frontal lobes, stimulates these voluntary motor functions. Certain actions involving skeletal muscles, however, are not commanded by the cerebrum but result from reflexive stimulation of the motor neurons in the spinal cord.

THE AUTONOMIC NERVOUS SYSTEM

From the contractions of the heart to the secretion of saliva, the actions of the visceral organs and the body's glands are controlled not consciously but through the autonomic nervous system. This system functions along two distinct paths. The sympathetic system of the autonomic nervous system goes through the spinal cord and a chain of ganglions, while its parasympathetic system mainly uses the nerve bundles of the vagus nerve (cranial nerve X).

SYMPATHETIC SYSTEM   PARASYMPATHETIC SYSTEM

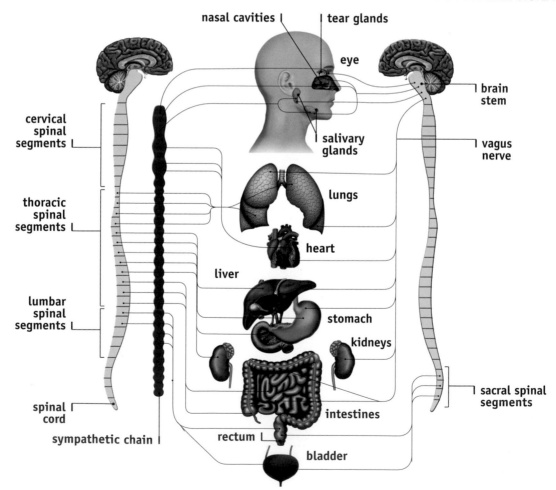

nasal cavities | tear glands

eye

brain stem

cervical spinal segments

salivary glands

vagus nerve

thoracic spinal segments

lungs

heart

liver

lumbar spinal segments

stomach

kidneys

sacral spinal segments

spinal cord

intestines

sympathetic chain | rectum

bladder

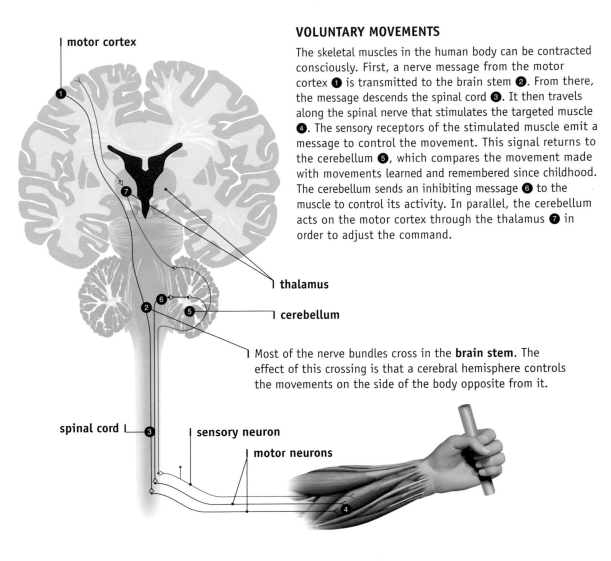

VOLUNTARY MOVEMENTS

The skeletal muscles in the human body can be contracted consciously. First, a nerve message from the motor cortex ❶ is transmitted to the brain stem ❷. From there, the message descends the spinal cord ❸. It then travels along the spinal nerve that stimulates the targeted muscle ❹. The sensory receptors of the stimulated muscle emit a message to control the movement. This signal returns to the cerebellum ❺, which compares the movement made with movements learned and remembered since childhood. The cerebellum sends an inhibiting message ❻ to the muscle to control its activity. In parallel, the cerebellum acts on the motor cortex through the thalamus ❼ in order to adjust the command.

motor cortex

thalamus

cerebellum

Most of the nerve bundles cross in the **brain stem.** The effect of this crossing is that a cerebral hemisphere controls the movements on the side of the body opposite from it.

spinal cord

sensory neuron

motor neurons

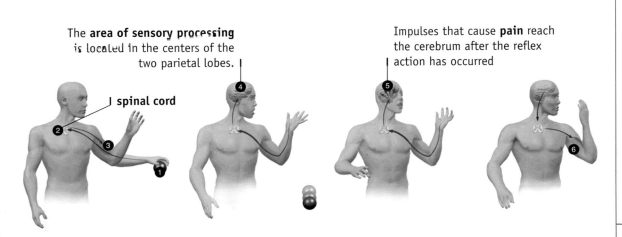

PAIN: REFLEX AND REACTION

When a hand picks up a very hot object ❶, receptors in the skin called nociceptors send a message to the spinal cord ❷. In just a few hundredths of a second, the spinal cord commands a muscular movement ❸ to release the object. This action is called a reflex. At the same time, other sensory nerves send a message to the area of sensory processing in the cerebrum ❹ to signal the sensation of touch. One or two seconds later, the nociceptor impulses arrive in the cortex, causing the sensation of pain ❺. Because the limbic system is also activated, emotions are felt, and the sensation is memorized. The cerebrum may then decide to order a conscious reaction ❻, such as blowing on the injury in order to inhibit the receptors and lessen the pain.

The **area of sensory processing** is located in the centers of the two parietal lobes.

spinal cord

Impulses that cause **pain** reach the cerebrum after the reflex action has occurred

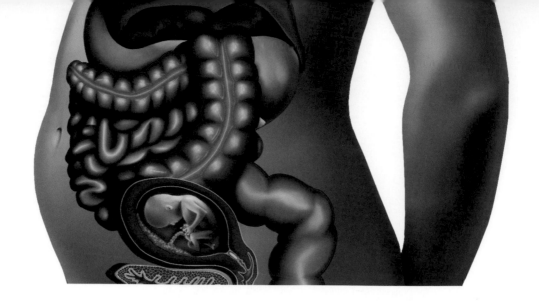

What are the anatomical and physiological differences between the male and female reproductive systems? How is the ovum fertilized by a spermatozoon? What is the difference between an embryo and a fetus, and what major steps do they go through in their development? How does childbirth take place? Because the human reproductive system is concerned with the transmission of life, it is particularly interesting.

Reproduction

Fertilization

The fusion of sexual cells

The male and female reproductive systems are complementary. Fertilization occurs when a spermatozoon, or male sexual cell, unites with an ovum, or female sexual cell. This union of cells usually happens as a result of sexual relations, and it brings together all the genetic material needed for the development of a new human being in the mother's uterus. The female reproductive system, however, makes an ovum available for fertilization only a few days each month before the ovum degenerates and is eliminated with the menstrual flow.

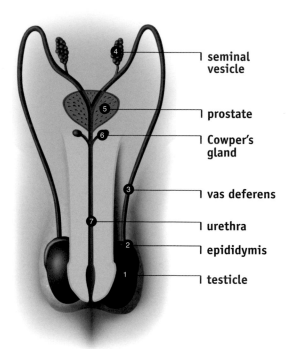

seminal vesicle

prostate

Cowper's gland

vas deferens

urethra

epididymis

testicle

THE PATH OF SPERMATOZOA

Spermatozoa, which are produced constantly by the testicles ❶, are stored while they mature in the epididymides ❷. When they flow up the vas deferens ❸, they combine with secretions from the seminal vesicles ❹, the prostate ❺, and the Cowper's glands ❻ to form a whitish liquid called semen. During sexual relations, semen is ejected through the urethra ❼ as a result of contractions of muscles at the root of the penis. Although semen contains countless spermatozoa, only one is needed to fertilize an ovum.

THE FEMALE REPRODUCTIVE APPARATUS

The ovaries are the female sexual glands; they produce the ova and the main sexual hormones. Two ducts, called the fallopian tubes, link the ovaries to the uterus, which is the muscular organ in which the embryo develops. The outer wall of the uterus is made of thick layers of muscle known as the myometrium. The cavity of the uterus is lined with a mucous membrane called the endometrium.

The uterus is connected to the vagina, a fibromuscular tube about 3 to 4 inches (7 to 10 cm) long at the level of the cervix. The vagina has very elastic walls in order to allow the baby to exit during childbirth.

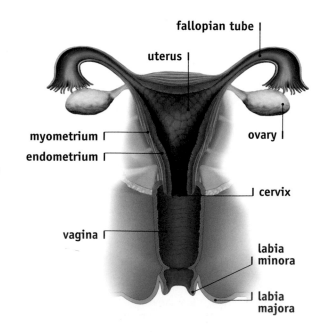

fallopian tube

uterus

myometrium

endometrium

ovary

cervix

vagina

labia minora

labia majora

THE MENSTRUAL CYCLE

Between puberty and menopause, a woman ovulates, or discharges an ovum from an ovary, between 400 and 500 times. Ovulation is the result of a cycle that lasts an average of 28 days. In the preovulatory phase, a follicle develops in one of the ovaries and releases estrogen that stimulates the endometrium, or the internal lining of the uterus, to thicken. The rise in estrogen level also causes the surge in the release of luteinizing hormone by the pituitary that causes ovulation.

Once the ovum is expelled into the fallopian tube, the follicle that produced it transforms into a corpus luteum. The corpus luteum secretes large quantities of progesterone and estrogen, which increase vascularization of the endometrium in order to prepare the uterus for a possible pregnancy. If the ovum is not fertilized, the corpus luteum degenerates after about eight days. The drop in hormone levels that results from the degeneration of the corpus luteum causes the blood vessels in the endometrium to constrict, and its top layer begins to detach 14 days after ovulation. A small amount of blood, mucus, and tissues—the menstrual flow—discharges out of the vagina for three to seven days. Then the cycle starts again.

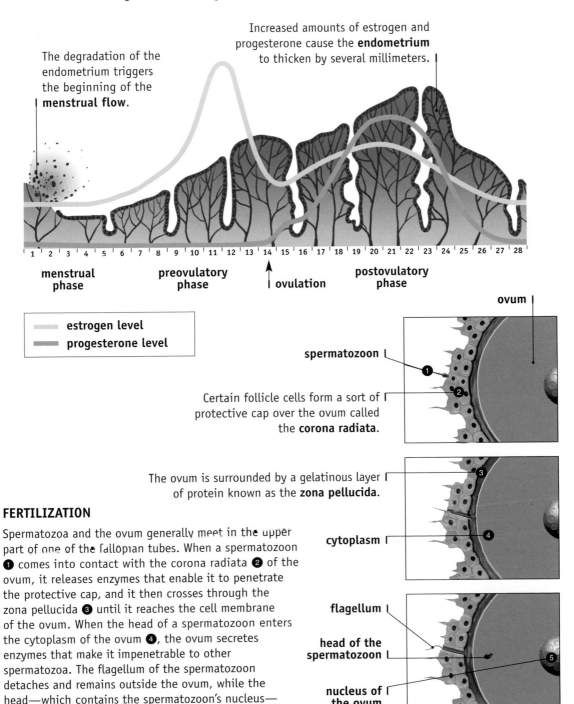

The degradation of the endometrium triggers the beginning of the **menstrual flow**.

Increased amounts of estrogen and progesterone cause the **endometrium** to thicken by several millimeters.

| 1 | 2 | 3 | 4 | 5 | 6 | 7 | 8 | 9 | 10 | 11 | 12 | 13 | 14 | 15 | 16 | 17 | 18 | 19 | 20 | 21 | 22 | 23 | 24 | 25 | 26 | 27 | 28 |

menstrual phase — **preovulatory phase** — ↑ **ovulation** — **postovulatory phase**

— estrogen level
— progesterone level

ovum

spermatozoon

Certain follicle cells form a sort of protective cap over the ovum called the **corona radiata**.

The ovum is surrounded by a gelatinous layer of protein known as the **zona pellucida**.

cytoplasm

FERTILIZATION

Spermatozoa and the ovum generally meet in the upper part of one of the fallopian tubes. When a spermatozoon ❶ comes into contact with the corona radiata ❷ of the ovum, it releases enzymes that enable it to penetrate the protective cap, and it then crosses through the zona pellucida ❸ until it reaches the cell membrane of the ovum. When the head of a spermatozoon enters the cytoplasm of the ovum ❹, the ovum secretes enzymes that make it impenetrable to other spermatozoa. The flagellum of the spermatozoon detaches and remains outside the ovum, while the head—which contains the spermatozoon's nucleus—unites with the nucleus of the ovum ❺.

flagellum

head of the spermatozoon

nucleus of the ovum

The Growth of the Embryo
The first weeks

During the first three months after fertilization of an ovum by a spermatozoon, the fertilized egg develops considerably and gradually transforms into a fetus—a being that looks human. Only 12 weeks pass between fertilization and the appearance of the future baby's fingernails.

FROM FERTILIZATION TO IMPLANTATION

The ovary ❶ releases the ovum into the fallopian tube ❷, where it encounters spermatozoa. When fertilization ❸ takes place, the nuclei of the ovum and a spermatozoon merge to form a single nucleus with 46 chromosomes. This fertilized egg cell, called a zygote ❹, divides immediately after fertilization and begins to descend the fallopian tube. The zygote's cellular divisions continue at a quickening pace, and after almost four days the zygote forms a solid ball of 16 cells known as the morula ❺. The next day, the morula enters the uterus and becomes a blastocyst ❻. Seven days after fertilization, the blastocyst attaches to the endometrium and implantation ❼ begins. Several days later, the blastocyst is completely buried in the endometrium, which supplies it with the nutrients it needs.

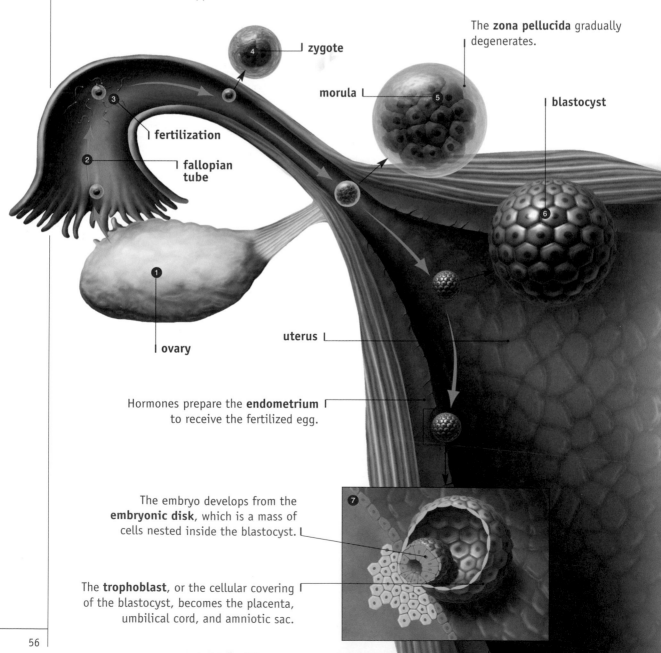

The **zona pellucida** gradually degenerates.

zygote

morula

blastocyst

fertilization

fallopian tube

ovary

uterus

Hormones prepare the **endometrium** to receive the fertilized egg.

The embryo develops from the **embryonic disk**, which is a mass of cells nested inside the blastocyst.

The **trophoblast**, or the cellular covering of the blastocyst, becomes the placenta, umbilical cord, and amniotic sac.

GROWTH OF THE EMBRYO

Two weeks after fertilization, the blastocyst is deeply anchored in the endometrium and the embryonic disk begins to develop; at this stage of development, the growing mass of cells is called an embryo. The systems of the body—including the nervous system and the cardiovascular system—develop after the first weeks, while the limbs are slower to develop.

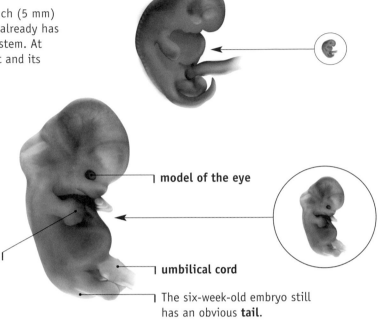

Even though it is only about .2 inch (5 mm) long, the **four-week-old embryo** already has a model of a spine and nervous system. At this stage, its heart begins to beat and its limbs begin to form.

At the end of the **sixth week**, the embryo is about .9 inch (22 mm) long. Its head, which is as big as the rest of its body, contains models for its eyes, ears, and mouth.

model of the eye

The arms develop and rudimentary **hands** appear.

umbilical cord

The six-week-old embryo still has an obvious **tail**.

THE FETUS

After eight weeks, the embryo has developed into a fetus. By this stage, it has begun to look more like a human baby, even though it is still only a little over 1 inch (3 cm) long and weighs only a few grams. During the rest of the pregnancy, the different organs of the fetus finish developing and its body grows considerably; a fetus' weight increases almost 1,000 times between the eighth week and birth.

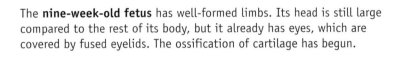

The **nine-week-old fetus** has well-formed limbs. Its head is still large compared to the rest of its body, but it already has eyes, which are covered by fused eyelids. The ossification of cartilage has begun.

At nine weeks, the **fingers** have separated.

Oxygen, nutrients, and antibodies pass into the fetus' body through the **umbilical cord**, which is composed of two arteries and one large vein.

At **12 weeks**, the fetus is between 2 and 3 inches (6 and 7 cm) long. Its face and its external ears become better defined, while its external genital organs become visible.

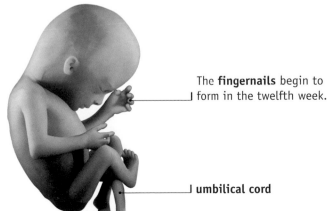

The **fingernails** begin to form in the twelfth week.

umbilical cord

Maternity

Reproduction

Gestation, childbirth, and nursing

During the nine months of gestation, the future baby develops inside the mother's body and is, therefore, totally dependent on her. The baby becomes physically separate from the mother at childbirth but remains deeply dependent on her, mainly through nursing.

NINE MONTHS OF GESTATION

In general, 40 weeks, or about 9 months, pass between fertilization of the ovum and childbirth. This period of time is called the gestation period. During the first three months, or the first trimester, of the pregnancy, the pregnant woman may experience nausea and her breasts begin to swell. In the second trimester, growth of the fetus causes the abdomen to swell. This related growth and swelling continues in the third trimester. The pregnant woman's heart rate and blood volume increase as the fetus develops, and so do her pulmonary volume and her appetite. Compression of the woman's internal organs caused by the size of the developing fetus may cause her minor physical problems, such as incontinence or heartburn.

FIRST TRIMESTER SECOND TRIMESTER THIRD TRIMESTER

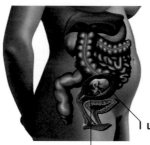

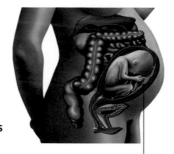
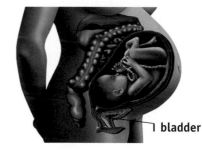

uterus

bladder

The **fetus** is surrounded by a liquid-filled pouch called the amniotic sac.

The **placenta** is a highly vascularized organ that forms against the wall of the uterus and provides nutrition for the fetus.

THE BREASTS

The breasts, which develop in girls at puberty, are mammary glands that cover the pectoral muscles and are surrounded by fatty tissue. Each mammary gland is formed of 20 lobes arranged in bunches. The breasts grow larger during pregnancy and produce milk after childbirth when stimulated by a hormone called prolactin. The lactiferous ducts route the mother's milk to reservoirs known as lactiferous sinuses, where it is stored until it is secreted through the tiny orifices of the nipples.

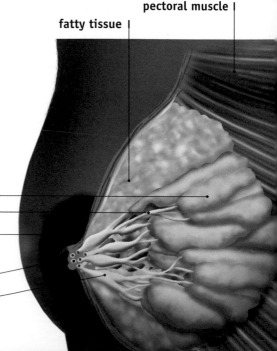

pectoral muscle

fatty tissue

Each **lobe** is connected to the nipple by a lactiferous duct.

lactiferous duct

The **areola**, which forms a circle around the nipple, contains sebaceous glands.

nipple

lactiferous sinus

CHILDBIRTH

In the weeks preceding childbirth, the fetus, which usually comes out head first, gradually descends between the bones of the pelvis and rests on the cervix.

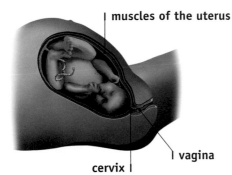

muscles of the uterus

cervix | **vagina**

DILATION

Childbirth begins when the combined action of a number of hormones provokes painful, rhythmic contractions of the uterus. These uterine contractions, which propagate from top to bottom, gradually dilate, or widen, the cervix and cause the amniotic sac to rupture.

EXPULSION

Several hours may pass before the cervix and vagina are sufficiently dilated to allow the baby to pass through. When the opening is about 4 inches (10 cm), the baby's head enters the vagina. With strong contractions of the mother's abdominal muscles, the child is expelled in less than an hour.

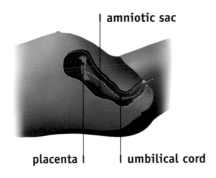

amniotic sac

placenta | **umbilical cord**

DELIVERY OF PLACENTA

After childbirth, the uterine muscles continue to contract in order to expel the placenta. These contractions also prevent hemorrhaging by compressing the damaged blood vessels. Complete retraction of the uterus and vagina may take several weeks.

NURSING

After childbirth, the mother can nurse her baby—nourish him or her with milk she produces in her breasts. Mother's milk is easily digestible, contains nutritive substances, and boosts the newborn's immune defenses. Stimulation of the nipples also provokes uterine contractions, which helps the uterus return to normal size.

The **baby's sucking** action is sensed by receptors in the mother's nipple. This information is transmitted to the pituitary gland, which secretes the hormones prolactin and oxytocin. Prolactin stimulates production of milk by the mammary glands, while oxytocin causes these glands to secrete the milk.

Glossary

abscess: A localized collection of pus surrounded by inflamed tissue.

acuity: Keenness of perception.

afferent: Describing the path of a nerve, vessel, or canal leading to an organ.

alimentary: Having to do with nutrition.

amplitude: The range of movement of a vibration above and below its average point.

apex: The tip of an organ.

aponeurosis: A sheet of dense connective tissue, resembling a tendon, that links a muscle to another muscle or to a bone.

bolus: A soft mass of chewed food.

commissures: Bands of tissue that join two parts of the body, especially in the brain and spinal cord.

cortex: The outside layer of an organ or bodily structure, especially the cerebrum, cerebellum, kidneys, and adrenal glands.

deciduous: Shedding or falling off at a certain stage of the life cycle.

dentition: The full set of teeth in an organism.

efferent: Describing the path of a nerve, vessel, or canal leading away from an organ.

endolymph: The potassium-rich liquid that fills the cavities of the inner ear and surrounds the organs of hearing and balance.

enzymes: Proteins that catalyze chemical reactions.

fetus: An unborn child at the stage after it has developed its basic structure.

follicle: A small pocket.

frequency: The number of periodic repetitions of a process in a unit of time.

ganglions: Masses of nerve tissue containing nerve cells external to the brain or spinal cord.

gustatory: Related to eating or the sense of taste.

histological: Having to do with tissue structure or organization.

innervated: Supplied with nerves.

juices: The natural fluids of an animal body.

membrane: A thin layer of tissue.

meninges: The three membranes that envelope the brain and spinal cord.

menopause: The period of natural cessation of menstruation.

metabolism: The physical processes in an organism by which it produces its substance and makes energy available within the body.

mucosa: A mucus-secreting membrane that lines an interior part of the body.

neurotransmitter: A substance that serves as a chemical messenger over the synapse that connects two neurons.

nociceptor: A nerve ending sensitive to pain stimuli.

occlusal: Having to do with the grinding or biting surface of a tooth.

olfactory: Having to do with the sense of smell.

organ: A part of the body made up of various kinds of tissues that has a definite shape and performs a particular function.

photoreceptor: A cell in the retina capable of converting light into nerve impulses.

propagate: To travel through a substance or space.

puberty: The period of life, generally between 11 and 16 years of age, during which the body changes to be able to reproduce.

regenerate: To restore to original strength or properties.

relay: A structure that serves to pass a signal from one area to another.

synaptic: Having to do with the point at which a nerve impulse passes from one neuron to another.

tunic: An enclosing or covering membrane or tissue.

vascularized: Having channels for the flow of blood.

Books

Atlas of the Human Body. Takeo Takahashi (Harper Collins)

The Big Book of the Brain: All About the Body's Control Center. John Farndon (Peter Bedrick Books)

The Digestive System (21st Century Health and Wellness). Regina Avraham (Chelsea House)

Eyewitness: The Human Body. Steve Parker (DK Publishing)

Incredible Voyage: Exploring the Human Body. (National Geographic Society)

The Nervous System (Encylopedia of Health: The Healthy Body). Edward Edelson (Chelsea House)

The Nervous System (Human Body Systems). Alvin Silverstein, Virginia Silverstein, Robert Silverstein (Twenty First Century Books)

The Reproductive System (Human Body Systems). Alvin Silverstein, Virginia Silverstein, Robert Silverstein (Twenty First Century Books)

The Respiratory System (21st Century Health and Wellness). Mary Kittredge, Sandra Thurman (Chelsea House)

Seeing (Senses and Sensors). Alvin Silverstein, Virginia Silverstein, Laura Silverstein Nunn (Twenty First Century Books)

Videos and CD-ROMs

The Brain and the Nervous System (Human Body in Action). (Schlessinger Science Library)

The Complete Human Body (CD-ROM). (Library Video)

Digestive and Excretory Systems (Human Body in Action). (Schlessinger Science Library)

Human Biology (CD-ROM). (Library Video)

Now Hear This: Vol. 12 (Body Atlas). (Library Video)

Taste and Smell: Vol.7 (Body Atlas). (Library Video)

Touch. (Nova)

Web Sites

3-D Brain Anatomy
www.pbs.org/wnet/brain/3d

BBC Science Sites: Human Body
www.bbc.co.uk/science/humanbody/
enhanced/index.shtml

How Hearing Works
gslc.genetics.utah.edu/thematic/
deafness/hearing/ear

The Nervous System
gened.emc.maricopa.edu/bio/bio181/
BIOBK/BioBookNERV.html

Index

Index